Jo and Laura Grimond

A Selection of Memories
and Photographs

1945 – 1994

EDITORIAL TEAM:
Jean Anderson, Barbara Foulkes,
Charles Tait, Ruth Williams and Rosie Wallace.

Text input and research mainly by Rosie Wallace,
scanning, image manipulation and captions by Charles Tait.

Front cover: Jo and Laura at the Old Manse - circa 1974
Back cover: Jo and Laura in the driveway of the Old Manse -
1984 (Gunnie Moberg)

Printed at The Orcadian Limited,
Hell's Half Acre, Hatston, Kirkwall, Orkney, KW15 1DW

ISBN 1-902957-09-1

September 2000

THANKS: to all who have contributed reminiscences, photographs and
anecdotes. Many people have assisted in the production of this book and the
editorial team wish to thank all who have taken part in its production.

CONTENTS

FOREWORD

When I was nine or ten years old I lived for a very brief period in the Lover's Leap Motel and Restaurant complex at Gretna Green, beside the busy A74. It was a favoured resting point for travellers and the staff there would frequently telephone the upstairs flat to alert me to the arrival of celebrities into the restaurant. Football players, pop stars, TV personalities quite frequently came under my gaze and filled my autograph book, and equally frequently left me disappointed - unable quite to fill the commanding figure which my mind's eye had created for them. Our expectations of our heroes can often fail to be matched by reality.

When, as an adolescent, I heard on TV and radio and read in newspapers and books the words of Jo Grimond I, like many at that time, was hooked. Here, I believed, was a man of passion, of flair, of leadership, of great vision, a man whose ideas struck a chord, both emotionally and ideologically; a politician who seemed to genuinely put the common weel before his own. Jo Grimond was the man whose vision led me to Liberalism and whose burning desire for Home Rule fuelled my own determination to see the creation of a Federal United Kingdom.

Many years later, when I met Jo - my first political hero - he more than lived up to my expectations. He was a big man in every sense of the word and his imposing presence was palpable as well as physical. When I first stood for Orkney and Shetland in 1983 I was new to the islands and unknown to the electorate. During my canvassing I was frequently met with the words: "If Jo says you're the man; then you're the man." His endorsement was most welcome; the depth of trust he had engendered among his constituents was, however, awe-inspiring. It is often a cliché used by new MPs to claim that if they could claim half the esteem of their predecessor, they would be happy. Half of Jo's esteem is more than many could even dream of – and popular ones at that. In her own less public way, Laura was the same. Her support for Jo was unswerving; her personal contribution to Liberalism immense. In many ways, Laura was the dynamo, the force which drove things on. Her single-minded determination was as inspirational as Jo's leadership and vision. As a team, they had the perfect balance. As a couple, they were warm and welcoming. As the tributes which follow suggest their deaths left unfillable gaps in many diverse lives. But what remains from their lives will kindle and rekindle the soul of Liberalism in hearts open and willing to let it enter.

Jim Wallace, August 2000

INTRODUCTION

February 2000 marked the 50th Anniversary of Jo Grimond's election to Westminster as MP for Orkney and Shetland. The Orkney Liberal Democrats felt that 50 years of Liberal and Liberal Democrat representation should not go unmarked and we decided to go ahead with a project we had started several years ago, namely to publish a book of reminiscences about Jo and Laura Grimond. We knew that both Jo and Laura had a profound effect on anyone they met and that people from Orkney, Shetland and the political world at large had a fund of memories and stories about them. This book is a collection of these memories, linked together by simple text. It does not aim to be a biographical account of this remarkable couple, merely a glimpse of how different people perceived them. We have used nearly all the contributions which were sent to us and have used as little editing as possible. We would like to thank all those who contributed to this book with reminiscences and photographs and also to the Grimond family for allowing us both to go ahead with this book and access to family photographs. Any modest profit, which may ensue from the sale of this book, will go towards ensuring that Orkney and Shetland continue to have Liberal Democrat representation at Westminster and Edinburgh for the next 50 years.

Jo Grimond

Born 29th July 1913 in St. Andrews, Fife, son of Joseph Grimond, Jute Manufacturer, and Helen Richardson.

Educated at Eton and Baliol College Oxford.

Called to the Bar Middle Temple 1937.

Married Laura Bonham Carter 1938.

Served 1939-45 Fife and Forfar Yeomanry and staff of 53rd Division and attained rank of Major.

Contested Orkney and Zetland in 1945 General Election.

Director of UNRRA 1945-47.

Secretary National Trust for Scotland 1947-49.

MP Orkney and Zetland 1950-83.

Leader Liberal Party 1956-67 and 1976.

Rector of Edinburgh University 1960-63 and Aberdeen University 1969-72.

Chancellor University of Kent 1970 -90.

Hon. Lld: Edinburgh 1960, Aberdeen 1972, Birmingham 1974, Buckingham 1983.

Hon. DCL Kent 1970, D.Univ. Sterling 1984.

Created Baron Grimond of Firth 1983.

Given Freedom of Orkney August 1987.

Died Kirkwall, Orkney, 24th October 1993

Jo and Laura as a young couple.

Laura Grimond

Born 13th October 1918 daughter of Sir Maurice and Lady Violet Bonham Carter (née Asquith).

Educated at home and in Vienna.

Married Joseph Grimond 1938.

Mother to 3 sons and 1 daughter.

Contested West Aberdeenshire 1970.

Orkney Islands Councillor (Firth and Harray) 1974-80.

President Womens' Liberal Federation and Chair of Liberal/SDP Defence Panel.

Founder member Orkney Heritage Society, Orkney Blide Trust, Hoy Trust and Sanday Development Trust.

Served as Honorary Sheriff in Orkney and Magistrate in Richmond.

Given Freedom of Orkney August 1987.

Died in Orkney 15th February 1994

Jo and Laura Grimond following their marriage in St Margaret's, Westminster in May 1938.

JO AND LAURA GRIMOND
1945 – 1956

In the early 1940s, Lady Glen-Coats, who had been the Liberal PPC for Orkney and Shetland, indicated that she would not stand at the next election and she recommended one Joseph Grimond as her successor. He was a Major in the Fife and Forfar Yeomanry and married with 2 small children. Jo did not expect to win Orkney and Shetland in the 1945 General Election. Basil Neven Spence, the sitting Tory MP, was expected to retain the seat, but Jo managed to get to most parts of the constituency and was well liked and respected by constituents whom he met.

Major Jo Grimond in the uniform of the Fife and Forfar Yeomanry when he first stood in 1945.

Mrs. Margaret Anderson, from the island of Whalsay in Shetland remembers Jo during that campaign.

"I was born and have lived on the island of Whalsay all my life. In the 1940s, the
M.V. Earl of Zetland arrived three times a week with supplies for the island. The
vessel anchored in South Voe, Symbister and a flitboat went off to bring goods and
passengers ashore - a hazardous journey indeed in bad weather when the "Earl'
had to anchor a long distance from the Voe. This is how Mr. and Mrs. Jo Grimond
would have arrived in Whalsay in the middle or late 40s or by fishing boat direct
from Lerwick.
Jo Grimond did quite a bit of walking round the island all those years ago and was
a popular and well-loved figure.
Prior to the 1950s all water used in the home was carried in buckets from
underground wells and water carrying was continuous. Each family carried water
from their nearest well, some having to walk quite a distance. There were no private
cars on the island in my youth, only a few vans belonging to local shops.
My school friends and I, on our long walks to and from Livister School, passed the
village of Whitefield twice daily. We often met Beenie, (Mrs. Laurie Simpson), and

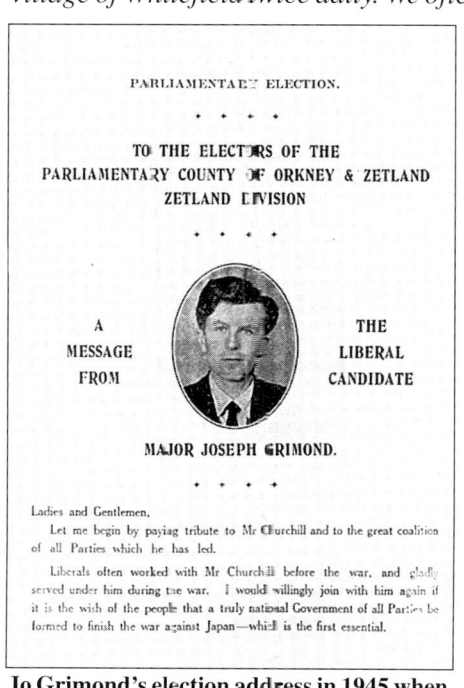

Jo Grimond's election address in 1945 when
he was within 329 votes of victory.

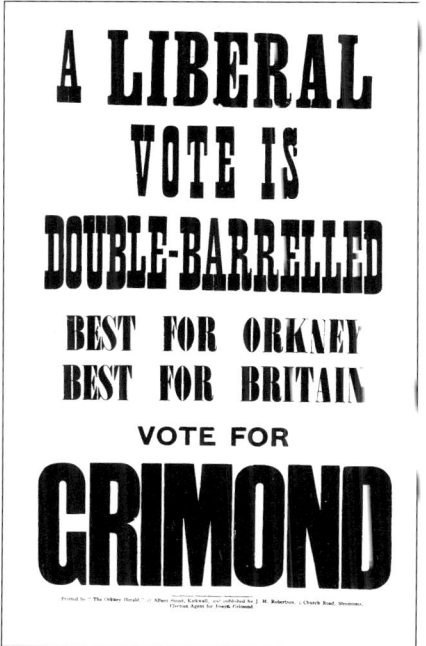

One of Jo Grimond's Election posters
from the 1945 General Election, a play on
the name of the Conservative opponent
Basil-Spence.

others in that area carrying water. Coming home from school one day we met Beenie as usual, but walking alongside her, carrying her two buckets of water was Jo Grimond. We knew he was trying to be our MP and that he must have walked quite a distance from the well. Arriving home from school we had some story to tell our parents that night.

Jo did not even attend the count and was very surprised to hear that he had come within 329 votes of victory. He admitted that he had spent too much time "taking tea with Tories" and had not been seen about the Constituency enough. Jo went back south to a job with the UN Relief and Rehabilitation Administration and then to become Secretary of the National Trust for Scotland.

The Constituency Associations in Orkney and Shetland were keen to have Jo as their candidate at the next General Election. There was a renewed enthusiasm amongst Liberal supporters and many of Jo's later supporters were recruited.

Mrs. Margaret Crossan MBE, from Lerwick, Shetland recalls

I joined the Liberals in 1947 when Mrs. Wishart (Basil's mother) formed a ladies committee which met in Peter Goodlad's office. We would make things for the handicraft stall for the Sale of Work to raise funds for the next Election campaign.

There was a correspondence spanning several years between Jo and the two Liberal Associations as the Orkney Liberal minute book recalls:

Extract from the minutes of the Orkney Liberal Association 18ᵗʰ February 1947 Mr. C.W. Tait in the chair:

"The secretary (Mr Edwin Eunson) was instructed to write to Major Grimond ....inviting him, in the name of the association to come forward again as the prospective Liberal candidate for the Constituency."

Jo was obviously not in a hurry to commit himself as the minutes of the meeting of 16ᵗʰ 'March 1948 record....

"The secretary reported that that he had not yet been able to ascertain whether or not Major Grimond would be in a position to contest the next election. He was instructed to write to Major Grimond again pressing for a definite reply.

By April 1949, Jo had decided to fight the seat. The minutes record that....

"Mr Joseph Grimond had accepted the invitations of the Orkney and Shetland Liberal Associations to become prospective candidate for the constituency and that he intended to come north in the summer months; this announcement being received with great enthusiasm.

PARLIAMENTARY ELECTION, 1950.

A MESSAGE TO

ORKNEY

FROM

YOUR LIBERAL CANDIDATE

JOSEPH GRIMOND

LADIES AND GENTLEMEN,

I again come to you as the Liberal candidate for this constituency, with the conviction that the considerable support which was accorded to me in 1945 and which brought me within 329 votes of victory, has been now reinforced by a large number of people who now realise that only through the Liberal Party can their Liberal ideals be achieved.

In asking you to consider the policy outlined within, I would also like to remind the younger members of the electorate of the great achievements of past Liberal governments, which some people appear to have forgotten. The principal rights of Trades Unions, Old Age Pensions, Unemployment and Sick Pay were all originally passed by Liberal governments, despite Tory opposition, though now the Tories try to claim credit for them.

If Liberalism is what you want, you will get it only by supporting the Liberal Party, and if you live in Orkney by giving me your vote on 23rd February.

Jo Grimond

VOTE LIBERAL FOR GRIMOND

Part of Jo's 1950 Election Address.

Liberal Orkney

A Man for the Islands

WHEN Joseph Grimond contested a constituency long unused to seeing its M.P. at any time other than elections, he said: "If you send me to Parliament I will make my home in the islands." This pledge was much more than an appeal to local sentiment, for Mr Grimond realised that no man could represent Orkney adequately who was not in touch with day to day affairs in the constituency. Thus it is that the M.P. has become a familiar figure in Kirkwall and Stromness and in the lovely village of Finstown where he now lives.

The outcome of this keen desire to become thoroughly familiar with island needs has been seen throughout the whole life of the Parliament just dissolved. The House had only been assembled for a few days, when the new member caught the Speaker's eye, and made an impressive maiden speech wholly occupied with the special concerns of Orkney and Shetland. The same conviction that local affairs, even the smallest local affairs, are his responsibility, has prompted him to focus the attention of the Mother of Parliaments, effectively, on issues which a lesser or lazier man would have neglected. Such matters as the North Ronaldshay radio link, the South Fara pier, or the state of broadcast reception in the islands, he has brought to the notice of authorities disposed to overlook them. Some idea of the work he has done during the short Parliament of 1950-51 may be gathered from the fact that he has made no less than fifty-three speeches, and that his total interventions in the House have numbered one hundred and seventy-four. Of the speeches, nine were devoted wholly to agriculture, six to transport and five to fisheries. Other subjects on which he has spoken trenchantly are Housing, the Cost of Living, Education, Pensions, Foreign Affairs and Defence.

Despite his concentration on matters of special interest to his constituents, Mr Grimond has not been silent on the great political issues which must finally mean as much to them as to the country at large. Local audiences have often remarked on the width of his interests and the range of his sympathies. His education (which included First Class Honours in Politics, Philosophy and Economics) enables him to see clearly and analytically the facts that so often get lost in the tangle of political debate, but he has never allowed logic to triumph over the humanities. His critics in Orkney often accuse him of appealing to the emotions. These forget that the bleak appeals to self-interest they so often hear from the platforms of Right and Left are not the only ones to commend themselves to men of goodwill. Mr Grimond is never afraid to allow the fire of his own generous sympathies to warm his speeches. These ardent sympathies have been seen also during the everyday business of Parliament. His hatred of cruelty was demonstrated in his interventions on behalf of homeless Greek children and of badly-treated children in our own country. His humanity also found expression in his plea for the famine-ridden masses of India, and his sense of justice in his disinterested backing of Seretse Khama and his uncle Tshekedi.

The Liberal attitude of taking principles to Parliament is to-day much misunderstood: it is sneered at as "the Nonconformist conscience." That is why the rival parties seek to make capital out of the fact that Mr Grimond has voted on each issue as his conscience dictated, rather than as the lumbering machines on either side of him desired. Happily this strong ethical sense has not yet been banished from Orkney, and will not be misunderstood here. As an example of our M.P.'s sense of fairness, two motions tabled in his name on the fifteenth of March last give ample demonstration:

(a) A motion asking the Government to institute an enquiry into unofficial strikes.

(b) A motion asking the Government to introduce general legislation making monopolistic practices unlawful.

There you have the failings of supporters of both the major parties brought up for criticism, a thing which is only possible where a free electorate send to Parliament a free representative, as Orkney had done.

Those who know Joseph Grimond well, know the laughter that is always lurking behind his kindly eyes. They know, too, how difficult it is to persuade him to return the devastating reply, which he is eminently capable of making, to the insinuations of his political rivals, for he hates wrangling and all the meaner forms of debate. His interest lies in making a wider, happier, nobler life for all through the instrument of democratic action, and on that ground he stands at this election, "a man of cheerful yesterdays and confident to-morrows."

> How happy is he, born or taught,
> Who serveth not another's will;
> Whose armour is his honest thought,
> And simple truth his utmost skill.

Jo Grimond, "A Man for the Islands."

LIBERAL ORKNEY

Sound Farming Policy

MR JOSEPH GRIMOND, prospective Liberal candidate for Orkney and Shetland, sends this message to 'Liberal Orkney.''

AGRICULTUEE is undoubtedly Orkney's major industry, and a period of national necessity has brought increased prosperity to our islands.

There is a legitimate fear in farming circles that this, as in former times, may be followed by a period of depression.

The Liberal Policy for agriculture seeks to remove this fear.

We are faced to-day with a world food shortage and rising population. Food experts consider that this gap between demand and supply is bound to continue. On this certainty a sound Agricultural Policy can be based.

(a) **LIVESTOCK.**
The breeding of livestock and poultry-breeding, for which Orkney is already famous, along with milk production, an increasingly important branch of farming, will receive the utmost consideration from a Liberal Government. There should be an extension of the policy of assured markets and guaranteed prices brought in by the war-time Coalition.

(b) **ORGANISATION.**
The Liberal aim is to establish a single department which would take over the functions of the various ministries which at present conduct agricultural affairs expensively and inefficiently.

(c) **SUBSIDIES.**
The present subsidy system does not properly distinguish between good farming and bad. The Liberal method would be to use subsidies as an incentive to greater production. Incompetent farmers would cease to share the rewards rightly given to the hard-working majority.

Controls would be reduced to a minimum, for the advantage of giving scope to personal initiative is fully recognised by the Liberal Party.

(d) **CROPS.**
No wheat is grown in Orkney, and it is urged that the growing of oats, our staple cereal product, should be made as profitable as the growing of wheat in other areas.

(e) **OTHER IMPROVEMENTS.**
We are alive to the necessity of keeping the people on the land. A great deal can be done to make life in the more isolated parts of the country more attractive than it is at present. A first step would be to encourage the man who wishes to improve his house by giving grants.

The provision of rural water-supplies would become a reality, the benefits of electricity would be made available to every home, and housing improvements would keep pace with these developments.

What We Stand For

LIBERALS believe that government exists for the people. We repudiate absolutely the tyranny of Communism or Fascism, or the idea of a society of classes such as lingers on in the Conservative Party. We refuse to resign our fate into the hands of civil servants however admirable.

To Liberals is due the very idea that the government should seek to raise the real value of wages and should look after the poor, the sick and the old. To them are due old age pensions, and unemployment insurance—to mention only two of their measures. The Liberal Party by the Crofters' Acts and their schemes for land settlement first envisaged the independent crofter and farmer.

The Liberal Party is determined to see that what they first won is defended and extended.

But they know that this cannot be done unless the country is energetic and enterprising and free from cant. We need a great united effort by everyone.

The Liberal Party puts forward a policy of encouragement to all enterprising and hard-working people, coupled with economy in government administration. It is a progressive policy which no other party can offer with sincerity.

Jo outlines the Liberals' "Sound Farming Policy" - 1950 General Election.

The 1950 campaign was fought with Jo taking "less tea with Tories" and holding meetings in nearly every parish and small island in Orkney and Shetland. Jo had his mother-in-law, Lady Violet Bonham Carter, to speak on his behalf in Orkney. The late **Rognvald Harvey** from Birsay told of a meeting in the old Dounby School:

"The chairman on that occasion was an elderly well known West Mainland farmer who at the end of the meeting rose to sum up.
"Surely" he said, ' this must be a good man when even his mother-in-law is speaking for him."

Jo was elected with a majority of 2,956 over Sir Basil Neven Spence with Harald Leslie (later Lord Birsay) for Labour in third place.
Jo had promised that if he were elected he would come and live in the constituency and in 1951 he and Laura purchased the Old Manse of Firth near Finstown in Orkney.

An aerial view of the Old Manse of Firth which Jo and Laura made their family home in 1951.

The late **David Eunson** recalled

In the 1950 campaign Jo made only one promise. If elected he would make his home in the constituency. He and his family had one or two temporary abodes before they bought the Old Manse of Firth. This purchase attracted great interest, and there was a prominent feature in the local press. Reactions in Orkney were interesting. The Liberals walked about with broad grins on their faces. The folk of Finstown, who were almost all Liberal anyhow, were absolutely delighted. Opponents tended to be snooty. It must be remembered that in those days so few Liberal candidates elsewhere put up even a respectable performance that many people, not only political opponents, thought that Jo's success in Orkney and Shetland would be short-lived. Those people expected that the Manse would be up for sale again fairly soon.

One diehard Tory lady in Kirkwall was especially disgusted when she saw the news of the purchase and was heard to exclaim,

"What's he daein'? He must think he's got a permanent job here!"

She was more or less right.

Jo was diligent in his work as MP and became widely respected within Orkney and Shetland. He seemed capable of putting everyone at their ease as **Robert Cursiter** from Quoyloo in Orkney remembers:

"From 1950 to the end of 1951 I was in Eastbank Hospital, Kirkwall, along with two other 16-17 year old lads. We had tuberculosis which was common in Orkney at that time.

One morning in what was probably April or May 1950, we had the pleasure of meeting Jo Grimond in Ward 6 of the Hospital. We learned later that he had visited every ward in the hospital and had a word with each patient. I still remember the ward door opening and the Sister introducing Jo Grimond to us three 16 and 17 year olds. He had on a tweed sports jacket, dark trousers and a patterned pullover and was not dressed in a suit like the specialists wore when they visited. This stopped us being nervous and made it easier for us to shake his hand and talk to him - being too young to vote or take an interest in politics at that time.

It did cheer us up to see him venture into the hospital and the TB ward which in those days was a dirty word and to be avoided at all costs. It was a talking point for us for a few days, as no other would risk coming to see TB patients.

The Grimond family outside the Old Manse of Firth shortly after moving in in 1951.
L to R Andrew, Johnny, Jo, Gelda & Laura.

When Jo and Laura moved to Orkney they brought with them their three children, Andrew aged 12, Gelda aged 9, and Johnny aged 3. An Orcadian accent can be quite difficult to follow for newcomers to Orkney and when a broad accent is combined with an unusual speech impediment, it can lead to communication problems as **Johnny Grimond** remembers

There was an occasion on which Mansie Flett came up to the Old Manse to paint some of the outside doors and windows. Mansie was a legendary figure in Finstown, not only for his joinery but also for his speech impediment: he could not help repeating the last few words of each sentence. Thus on a bright morning he would remark: "Come a fine day, a fine day, a fine day. " Or he would ask: "what has two hookers, two lookers, four dilly-danglers and a fling-by, a fling-by, a fling-by?" (The answer was a cow.) On this occasion, in the garden, he picked up a potato and inquired: "Good date, good date, good date? " This was in the 1950s, and deafness had not begun to afflict my father seriously. Nonetheless he was baffled, and indicated as much. But every time he tried to find out what Mansie was getting at, the question would merely be repeated — and repeated and repeated and repeated, embarrassment adding an extra "Good date?" or two on each occasion. Only on the umpteenth "Good date?" did my father realise that Mansie was asking whether the potatoes were good to eat.

The hub of Jo's Orkney election campaigns was a house in Victoria St., Kirkwall owned by Mrs. Eunson whose grandson **David Partner** remembers the comings and goings.

From 1950 onwards, the house became the centre of Liberal politics in Orkney. The year Jo was elected, I was approaching my 10th birthday and I can remember Jo holding his consultations there. Many people came to see him and sometimes I would be dispatched by my grandmother to go and open the door and show them upstairs. There was a large dining room upstairs which was a suitable room for the Liberals to use as a Committee Room. At Election times, there would be several thousand election addresses all waiting to be folded, envelopes, posters and all the paraphernalia of elections. There could be up to 15 people in the room at any one time working against the clock to get the envelopes stuffed so that they could be dispatched to the post office for delivery.
My grandmother came into her own when it came to making tea, which was brewed in the back kitchen and carried upstairs to the workers. After tea was over there was a rush to the kitchen sink to wash up and foremost in that rush was Laura. My grandmother found an affinity with Jo and Laura through their mutual love of gardening and at non election times, they would walk through the garden discussing plants and flowers and exchanging cuttings.

Jo and his right-hand man, Edwin Eunson, discuss strategy for the 1951 General Election. (courtesy Edwin Eunson).

1951 saw another election and Jo was re-elected with a hugely increased majority of 6,391. Jo was now the only Liberal MP in Scotland and Chief Whip of the Party and spent his time trying to hold together 6 very individual members who did not all get on with each other.

Conrad Russell recalls a misprint from the end of Jo's period as Chief Whip.

Jo was the subject of my very favourite newspaper misprint. This was in 1956, in the Guardian, before it became the 'Grauniad.' It read, "The amendment stands in the name of Mr. Joseph Grimond, the Liberal Chief Whop." I had the great pleasure of drawing Jo's attention to this misprint 35 years later and listening to his laughter echoing around the House.

In Shetland, the home of Jim and Margaret Crossan provided a base for Jo from his earliest days as MP. **Margaret** recalls:

I can remember Jo coming to our house in Burra Rd during one of the election campaigns in the 50s. He would have his tea with us and then go out to various halls to speak at the election meetings. I also remember him sitting with our children Kathleen and Kenneth watching children's TV programmes and paying no attention to the people who had come round to the house to discuss political issues. He told me it was one of the best evenings he had spent in a long time.

Jo landing at Papay during campaigning in the early 1950s. Travelling around an islands constituency is not always easy!

Elections were not without trials in the 1950s especially in the Northern Isles. The late **David Eunson** was the chairman at one meeting in Stromness in Orkney.

Election meetings in the old Stromness Town Hall used to be fairly lively events. They were well attended, and all speakers were heard with courtesy, but questions were never slow in coming and on occasion could be fairly hostile. Some questioners seemed to think that the audience had come to hear the brilliance of their questions rather than of the candidate's replies. However it was noteworthy that these people, like everybody else, would always join in the vote of thanks at the end.
One Election meeting there stands out in the memory. As I was to take the chair I arrived early, to find the hall-keeper, the agent (Jackie Robertson), and the police in earnest consultation. Jackie did not seem his normal self; he appeared out of

breath and somewhat flustered. It turned out that the police had come to warn us that there was going to be a power-cut all over Stromness in a matter of minutes. Jackie had hastened to J.D.Towers' shop and bought some candles, remembering to get a receipt for them, which was later included in the election expenses. Someone else had produced candlesticks. So at least Jo would be able to see his notes. By the time he arrived we were as ready as we could be.

Jackie Robertson, the Stromness solicitor, who was Jos agent throughout the 1950s and 1960s. It was Jackie who coined the phrase "Vote for Jo – the man you know".

Soon after Jo began to speak the lights duly went off. The meeting carried on with the only illumination coming from a few candles on the platform. Nobody was put off, least of all Jo.

In the 1955 General Election Jo's majority was nearly 8,000 and he now seemed to have a safe seat. Even outwith elections, Jo and Laura managed to visit Orkney's North isles regularly. **The Rev and Mrs. Fox**, from Stronsay remember two visits in 1955.

Mr. and Mrs. Grimond visited Stronsay many times and were frequent visitors at the Manse. In May 1955, the Moncur Memorial Church was dedicated and Laura Grimond as a representative of the trustees unveiled the memorial tablet while the Moderator of the General Assembly pronounced the words of the dedication and then in August 1955, Laura Grimond named the new lifeboat.

JO, LEADER OF THE LIBERAL PARTY

1956 – 1967

In 1956 Jo who had been Chief Whip for five years became Party Leader on the retiral of Clement Davies and thus Jo the National Politician was born.

Sarah Curtis was a student at Oxford at that time.

When Jo Grimond took the leadership of the Liberal Party at the Llandudno Party Assembly in the autumn of 1956 we knew that once again the nation would listen to the voice of liberalism It was not that the principles, the attitudes or even the policies would change, and Clement Davies held the respect and indeed the affection of the party. The difference was that in Jo we had a communicator of genius, who could put into words for a new generation both the idealism and the pragmatism of Liberal beliefs.

I was cheering at that Assembly, then aged twenty and the newly elected President of Oxford University Liberal Club. Perhaps as one of the few young women on the scene, once I had made it clear that I didn't want just to cut sandwiches, I found no difficulty in getting elected to student or Party offices - I was asked to say on BBC television news that night what the reaction of young people would be to Jo as leader. "He's marvellous," I said. "They'll love him".

I then went back to Oxford to prove it was true. At that time the posters on which the various political clubs advertised their events and through which they recruited members consisted of restrained lines of type, laid out by a helpful printer. Ours was at least blue on bright yellow but it didn't exactly sing. I decided that our poster for the Michaelmas Term, the crucial term in which the political clubs tried to recruit from the new intake of students, many of whom might join more than one club just to see what they all offered, would be different. Instead of a long list of our meetings it would carry a big black and white photo of Jo, the one in which he looked at you firmly but slightly quizzically with that loose lock of hair on his forehead. Underneath it just said "Join OU Liberal Club and hear Jo Grimond" or something like that. I don't know whether it was the poster that did it or the general aura of excitement that Jo had generated from the start but that term the Liberals were the biggest Oxford political club with over 1,000 members. This was a time, remember, when we were down to six MPs and Liberals were thought of as vague, well-meaning but irrelevant relics of the past. I'm not saying that all those who joined and came to the

Jo pictured at the time he became leader in 1956 (Sunday Times – Douglas Glass).

meeting at which Jo spoke became life-long Liberals, although Richard Holme, now Lord Holme of Cheltenham, was one of those recruited at that time. But I am sure that from then on they will all have considered the Liberal alternative.

And what an attractive alternative it was, as elucidated, interpreted and transmitted by his first-class mind and in his firm but always slightly humorous manner. When he came to Oxford, as we walked down the staircase at the Union to the debating chamber - I took the chair by courtesy of my Secretary as women, despite our regular protestations, were still not allowed to belong - he said in that low-key, almost flippant, off-the-cuff way he had, "Of course, in the end there'll always be conservatives but the real socialists will be reduced to a small rump". He was right, though New Labour still don't see how conservative they are.

Jo saw that the Party had to attract young people if it was to grow and it was one of his strengths that he trusted young people and listened to them before it was fashionable to do so. He included young people like me who were in their twenties on his Political Advisory Committee as well as those with experience. He practised what he preached about the need for openness and development. The tiny Party research department was much used and encouraged by him, producing inter alia work on employment and welfare which was far ahead of its time. But what I soon learnt was that it wasn't only to the young or the intellectuals that Jo appealed. He was at ease with everyone, able to talk, joke and get his message across all barriers of class and age. He really seemed to listen to people and it thus was particularly cruel that he grew deaf in his seventies. He had the gift of being able to put his complicated, sophisticated political creed in words that were totally comprehensible to all, yet he didn't distort by simplification. His rhetoric worked "I intend to march my troops towards the sound of gunfire" - but it wasn't meretricious. Perhaps he managed it because he had such a lucid as well as original mind.

Re-reading his 1959 book "The Liberal Future", his toughness as well as his clarity shine out. "Reason, " he says, "so far from being a rather ordinary little flower which Liberals along with everyone else wear in their button-holes, is a nettle for Liberals to grasp." Thus faith and Liberal principles must be discussable and be willing to submit to empirical tests. Jo was no head-in-the-clouds theorist but an essentially practical politician. I still like the notion that "Reasonable Liberals must have a touch of spleen to make their reasonableness bite."

Jo pictured with President Kennedy at the White House (Associated Press).

The life of a Party Leader does not always run smoothly and Johnny Grimond remembers an embarrassing incident which occurred when Jo was on a visit to the United States not long after he became leader.

This occurred on one of my father's first trips to America. He was staying with friends in New England, and it was cold, extremely cold. But, this being America, the house was centrally-heated and double glazed, and my father's bedroom was uncomfortably hot. In the middle of the night, unable to sleep, he decided to take action. First he tried to turn off the radiator, only to find that he could not. The next step was to open the window, or rather windows, first the inner one, then the outer. Kneeling down, in order to get more leverage, he had just managed to raise the second one when the first descended, pinning both his arms to the sill. As he struggled vainly to extricate himself, half his body was pressed to the red-hot radiator beneath the window, while his hands and forearms slowly turned blue with cold. Dawn was still several hours away.

1959 brought not only another Election but it also brought the arrival of Magnus, who was out electioneering from an extremely early age in a pram covered in *Vote for Jo* posters. But the 1959 election was different from the previous ones. As Party Leader, Jo had to be away from the Constituency for some of the campaign as he toured the country. The late **Basil Wishart** from Shetland was Jo's aide in this election and before his death he wrote about the last week of that campaign

Jo campaigning at the Market Cross, Lerwick with Basil Wishart (Dennis Coutts).

When the 1959 General Election seemed imminent, Liberal HQ planned a considerable programme for the Party Leader which Jo whittled down to a whistlestop tour in election week. He had asked me to accompany him on this trip and I became a self-styled PRO for a few memorable days.

"Why are you spending so much of your time in your own constituency?" asked the "Guardian" man at a Press conference in the National Liberal Club on the Saturday morning.

"Do you realise that the length of my constituency is about the same as the distance between London and Doncaster?" Jo countered.

Jo asked me where I was staying, adding that their London house was "....a bit of a shambles. There was a mouse running over the kitchen table yesterday ."

When I said I was staying at the National Liberal Club he said he didn't realise I was a member.

*"I'm not but Party workers are made honorary members at election time" I said.
"That's very decent of them," said Jo. "I'm not a member myself."
He went on to tell how F .E. Smith (Lord Birkenhead) used to come in the side door
of the club as he walked to the House from Charing Cross station. After using the
basement lavatory, he was leaving by the front door when he was confronted by a
Liberal MP 'Good God, Smith, what are you doing here? This is the Liberal Club,"
he said.
"Is it?" said Smith, "I thought it was a public lavatory."
We moved over to Liberal headquarters where Frank Byers was in unmistakable
command. Jo was ushered into a private office where he dictated the television
speech he was to make that night. Two secretaries took dictation, emerging
alternately at intervals with a typed page. This produced anguished cries such as
"That's not Party policy" and "He must say something about pensions" but there
were tedious silences.
 Jo did his own thing, his own way, and only his devoted secretary, Catherine Fisher,
knew what was in his diary. I have known Laura to phone from Orkney, asking "Is
Jo with you? I thought he was going to Shetland." More serious was the fact that,
after a TV appearance in Scarborough, he had accepted a lift back to London in a
Tory MP's car. He had ruminated and pondered over politics and personalities
unmindful of the fact that there was a third man, in the back seat. Alas, he was a
journalist and noted what Jo had thought were entertaining confidences, not
political indiscretions. He ought to have an ADC or private secretary with him to
prevent a similar gaffe and to smooth the path for him, I told Frank Byers. That
the latter acted solely on my advice I doubt, but years later when I told Jo he said,
"So it was your fault? It took me six months to get rid of the chap."
At the television centre at Wembley Jo had to read chunks of his speech over and
over again while it was typed onto the auto-cue but at one stage he looked at the
last page and said "I don't like that. I should change it. What do you suggest?"
That the man should discard his peroration left me speechless.
"Come on Wishart!" he said. "Why do you think I brought you here?" Then,
shuffling the typescript together, he sat before the cameras and, ignoring the auto-
cue, concluded in a different vein and at greater length. At such length that ITV
cut him off when they ran out of time for the adverts.
A helicopter had been chartered at great expense to an impoverished minority
party to fly the Leader to the Far West on Sunday but Jo had his own itinerary. He
would take the night train to Cornwall. Thus I had one splendid day posing as a VIP,
the sole passenger in a whirlybird. We landed at the RAF field at St Mawgan and
I spent the night in nearby Newquay, rising long before dawn to meet the train at
Bodmin. Jo nagged on about newspapers and before breakfast I got the porter to*

go out and buy the lot. *Generous in large degree he was, like many of his kind, frugal in minor matters.*

"Don't you think we should give that porter half-a-crown" he suggested. I told him I'd already given the man a pound and put it on the Leader's expense account. The day was a whirl of landings, car cavalcades, jeep rides and take-offs. Early evening brought us to Manchester for a swift visit to a Liberal club whose beerswilling members gave lip support to an obvious local loser and then - with a police escort, no less, and blaring sirens - to Rochdale where Ludovic Kennedy was holding forth to a crowded town hall. The organ blared "See the Conquering Hero comes" as Jo strode onto the platform. I thought Ludo would make it! He did well to cut the Labour majority from 4530 at the 1958 by-election to 2740 but I was disappointed. I found solace in a story - doubtless apocryphal - that circulated after that first attempt. Jo met Kennedy's dazzling young wife after the meeting. "Hello, Moira. What are you doing here?" he asked. "Helping Ludo" she replied. "What, canvassing? Knocking on doors asking people to vote for your husband? How frightfully embarrassing!"

From Rochdale we were driven through the night in a chauffeured Daimler to Glasgow where we caught the morning flight to Shetland via Orkney. At Grimsetter Laura dashed into the terminal, her hair streaked with paint and a swatch of carpet samples in her hands. "We must choose a dining room carpet" she announced. Reluctantly laying down the "Guardian", her husband flicked through the Wiltons and Axminsters and amiably remarked "I've heard some of that rubber-backed stuff is quite good." She headed back to the Old Manse of Firth before we took off for Sumburgh. At the weekend we learned that Jo had gone back to Westminster with an increased majority.

After the 1959 Election, there were still only 6 MPs. Mark Bonham Carter lost the seat he had won at a by-election the year before and Jeremy Thorpe won North Devon. **Jeremy Thorpe** remembers a Party Political Broadcast made soon after that

I remember one occasion when the entire parliamentary party of six gathered at the BBC studios to do a Party Political Broadcast. As a backdrop, there was a large map of the UK and just before we started, Jo roared: "Stop it. Stop it. You have left out my Constituency. You sit on your bottoms in London thinking you own the world, whilst in fact Britain's new wealth in oil is found in the North Sea. You must add Orkney and Shetland or I'll not take part in the programme." It was done. The BBC was duly chastened.

The Liberal Ball, December 1960. Seated around the table are Jo & Laura Grimond, Arthur &Kath Holt, Richard & Joyce Wainwright, Philip Fothergill and Joy Fothergill-Smith.

While Jo was touring the country preaching Liberal philosophy, one of his youngest constituents in Orkney had his welfare at heart. The late **David Eunson** related the following story.

As is well known, teachers do not always get the answers they are expecting. One Primary teacher in Stromness was taking a lesson in Religious Education. It dealt with someone in the Bible who was giving thanks to God in prayer. Enlarging on the subject she suggested that they should all think of people and things that they themselves should thank God for. She got quite a long list - mothers, fathers, homes, food, clothes, etc. Just before leaving the subject she asked, "Anyone else you can think of?"
One small boy had a sudden inspiration, shot up his hand and exclaimed, "What aboot Jo Grimond? We must no' forget him!"
The teacher accepted this addition to the list.

When other girls were collecting pictures of pop stars, **Kim Foden** was amassing a scrapbook of pictures of Jo.

"Cliff or Elvis?" "Jo" I'd offer. "No. You can't say him. Cliff or Elvis?"
At times (election times) there was a buzz in the Twatt household and Jo was the centre of it all. Dad, Jack Twatt, was part of an Action Committee. (I had never thought of him as an Action Man.) There were photos of Jo and family, lots of writing to be done proofs to read and endless meetings to attend. I was little but tried to tag along - for a glimpse of Jo.
Gran, and Grandad Gibb lived in Glasgow and all too often Elissa, my sister, and I were sent with B.E.A. to visit them. A scary trip for two peedie lasses although Big Sis would never

Jack Twatt, editor of the Orkney Herald, and a staunch Liberal, with Jo and Magnus on Kirkwall Pier in the 1960s.

admit that. To hear Jo's reassuring voice in the Nissan hut at Grimsetter Airport would be a huge relief. He took us under his protective wing on many a trip. A large, smiling, dependable man whom everyone knew, and who knew everyone. He'd get us there, no messing and everything would be O.K.
Jo Grimond, my Superstar.

During his period as leader Jo's charisma and eloquence brought many people into the Liberal Party. One of these was **Monroe Palmer** from Rye:

It was Jo Grimond who brought me into the Liberal Party in the early 1960s. His views expressed then on the rights of individual and the building up and protection of communities separated us from the other Parties and that difference is still there today.

Jo Grimond on the pier at Burra Isle talking to Mr Riddle, Headmaster of the Hamnavoe School on 29 Sept 1962 (Chris Holroyd).

That is a statement which could be made by many members of the Party today, but perhaps most strongly by **Edwin Eunson,** who was for many years Jo's chairman in Orkney and who was responsible for persuading Jo to stand again in the 1950 election. He recalled to Jim Wallace that during the crucial debate at the Assembly about whether or not the Liberals should form an Alliance with the SDP he had put in a card to speak.

Having heard all these people say how they'd been brought into the Party by Jo, I thought it would give some historic perspective if I'd been able to tell them how I had been the one to persuade Jo to stand again for the Party.

Jo was always ready to support a cause if he thought it was right and by so doing gained respect and affection from those of all political persuasions and none. An example of this was **Tony Benn's** fight to remain an MP when he inherited a peerage

Jo came to speak for me in Bristol in 1961 when I was fighting an election against my disqualification as a Member of Parliament because of my Peerage. I knew him well and I will never forget his kindness.

Leader of the Liberal Party, Jo Grimond, arriving at Hamnavoe in Shetland on 29 Sept 1962 to speak about the Common Market. (Chris Holroyd).

Colne Valley by-Election 1963 – Jo Grimond speaking at Skelmanthorpe with Richard and Joyce Wainright and their youngest daughter, Tessa.

It is the job of a Party Leader to campaign vigorously in mid term by-elections and **Richard Wainwright** was a candidate in such a by-election in 1963 and later became MP in 1966.

The 1963 Colne Valley by-election was electrified in three ways: the first voting test of Wilson's succession to Gaitskell, the desperate economic plight of the Tory government, and how far Liberals could repeat in a Labour seat their 1962 triumph in Tory Orpington.

So Holmfirth's largest hall was packed full for Jo's by'-election visit. In top form he stirred an initially sceptical crowd ("we've all heard for ages this talk of Liberal revival") ; and never once from Jo any fashionable but meaningless gimmick phrase. But people were manifestly waiting for their question time. After a couple of friendly questions there came a rasping voice: "What will Mr. Grimond do for the working class?" Jo uncoiled himself and summoned up his matchless gift of commanding emphasis; and then just one sentence: "'The working class - I would abolish the working class". Several seconds for his nine-word answer to sink in, and then huge applause, not from Liberals only. And no come back from the well-known Labour questioner.

The milling crowd at the hall-door, eager to shake Jo's hand, showed that a large public meeting with a superb speaker and lively questions can affect voters in a fashion TV cannot match. Three years later Colne Valley elected a Liberal MP.

Lord McNally remembers the impact Jo made on him in a TV debate.

Like many of my generation Jo Grimond was the Liberal Party and a mighty attractive personification he was too. I remember watching him debate with Bob Boothby and Dick Crossman on an early evening political programme which no television company would dream of putting out now and enjoyed his civilised manner and sound common sense.

Jo also managed to find time to speak at meetings within his own constituency although not to the same packed halls, but still leaving a definite impression on the audience. **Mrs. Joey Johnson** from Lerwick was at such a meeting.

On a bitterly cold ice-bound Saturday afternoon during the time of the Cold War, Jo Grimond was billed to give an address on his experiences in the Eastern Bloc countries which he had just been visiting. There were five of us in the audience in the Town Hall that memorable afternoon including Jo's agent Basil Wishart. Well, Jo Grimond stood before us and spoke brilliantly and humourously about his travels as if there had been a full house. I admired him so much.

Jo Grimond, Liberal Leader at Orpington in 1964, celebrating the famous by-election victory of Eric Lubbock the previous year.

The Grimond family at home in the Old Manse of Firth in 1964. L to R Laura, Jo, Magnus, Johnny, Gelda and Andrew (Sinclair's Studio).

As Jo's fame and popularity grew nationally, at home in the Constituency there was a feeling of pride in his achievements as well as a feeling of affection that one would reserve for an old friend. The late **David Eunson** related the origins of Jo's famous election slogan in Orkney and Shetland

"Vote for Jo, the man you know!"
It is said that when Jackie Robertson, the Liberal Election Agent heard some small boys shouting this slogan on the streets of Stromness, he said to himself with justifiable self satisfaction, "Ah, fame at last!" Jackie was adept at thinking out slogans and catch phrases and this turned out to be his most famous and successful. It is received wisdom that political or advertising slogans should be changed regularly in case they bore people by repetition. There are however admitted to be a few exceptions to this rule, sayings which go on and on, and never lose their impact. There is for example the whisky advertisement which warns drinkers against

Jo at the building site of the new Council housing estate in Lerwick talking to Jock McConnon in 1964 (Dennis Coutts).

vagueness. In politics in Orkney and Shetland this slogan was similar in that respect. At one election the Tories tried to respond in similar vein. They produced a slogan, "Don't fiddle - BanJo." This however did not have the simplicity and direct appeal of the Liberal one, and went down like a lead balloon. It was not used again. In his speech after the declaration Jo thanked the people of Orkney and Shetland for not discarding the native fiddle for the alien banjo.

Lord Mackie of Benshie who as **George Mackie** was Liberal MP for Caithness and Sutherland from 1954 –66 (when he lost the seat to the Labour candidate, one Robert MacLennan) remembers Jo campaigning with him in both these elections.

During the '64 and '65 Elections, Jo did an enormous amount of work in the Highlands and this was much appreciated by me as Chairman of the Organisation Committee and personally, as potential Member for Caithness and Sutherland. My Headquarters was the Portland Arms Hotel in Lybster run by two very good friends, Bert and Elizabeth Mowatt. After a long day of meetings and canvassing, Jo and I arrived back at the Portland Arms Hotel at about 1.30 a.m. We found,

Jo getting to know the ropes on board MV "Serene" in Whalsay with Theodore Kay, Robbie John Anderson and Willie Anderson (Dennis Coutts).

Jo with Russell Johnston and George Mackie on the publication of the Liberal Highland Development pamphlet in 1963. This was the blueprint for the Highlands and Islands Development Board which was established in 1965.

waiting for us in the fridge, a bottle of excellent Hock and a lobster each with mayonnaise. We tucked in and when we finished Jo leaned back into his chair and said, "I must persuade the Mowatts to move to Orkney!"

The 1966 election was the last one which Jo fought as Leader. **Michael Meadowcroft** who was to become a Liberal MP in 1983 was a key worker in the election campaign.

At the 1966 General Election, I was in charge of the HQ end of Jo's Leader's tours. We had installed a special hotline at HQ – at that time in Victoria St. roughly where Westminster City Council building now is – and this phone flashed red whenever , Jo's aide, Keith phoned me.
We had hired a light plane and Jo's first excursion was to the West Country. Keith and Jo and Jo's secretary Catherine Fisher – the only person who could read Jo's handwriting – duly set off to Heathrow to fly to RAF Chivenor. As the scheduled time for departure

Jo Grimond presenting the Party's General Election Manifesto, entitled "For All the People" at the Liberal Party HQ in London, 10 Mar 1966. (Central Press Photo).

passed, I relaxed, at least an hour's flying time to go. Suddenly, the red light flashed. It was Keith.
"We're delayed at Heathrow. Cancel the first meeting at Chivenor."
I protested mildly but to no avail. I then asked, "Keith, have you told the authorities at Heathrow that there is a General Election on and that you have a Party Leader on board?"
He replied that he hadn't. I suggested that it might speed things up a little if he mentioned it.
I took a deep breath and phoned Lilian Prowse, Jeremy Thorpe's formidable agent

1966 Liberal Party Conference, Brighton 21 Sept 1966. Leader of the Liberal Party, Jo Grimond pictured with Lord Byers. (Sport & General Press Agency).

in North Devon. "Lilian, We've got a problem. Jo is delayed at Heathrow and you'll have to cancel the rally at Chivenor."

Another long pause. "OK, fine." said Lilian.

Surprised to get such a cooperative response, I again relaxed. But then eventually, Keith rang again. "I thought I told you to cancel the rally ay Chivenor"

"I did."

"Well, short of mowing down 500 voters, we had to stop and address them."

I realised immediately Lilian's shrewd assessment of the situation when I phoned. Keith went on "Cancel the meeting at Bideford so that we can get back on schedule." Learning swiftly the Prowse technique, I agreed immediately and phoned Noel Penstone the Torrington Division agent. Noel, not being as experienced as Lilian, protested vehemently as I told him the facts of a leader's tour life.

Keith's next call was somewhat later. "Michael, where are we lunching in Collumption?"

"The guide will tell you."

"What guide?"

"The guide you picked up in Bideford."

It turned out that Keith rightly fearing a repeat of the Chivenor episode had taken a diversion around Bideford.

What happened next, was related to me by Catherine Fisher. Apparently, Keith returned to the limousine containing the Liberal Party leader in the middle of a General Election campaign becalmed in an apparently depopulated Devon village, got into the car and sat there not saying a word. Eventually, Jo demanded an explanation and got it. Jo then said " This demands action" got out of the car and approached the sole remaining inhabitant of Collumption quietly sitting on his doorstep and demanded where he was due to lunch. The startled Devonian directed Jo to the local pub which duly produced a sandwich or two. To this day, I reckon there's a loyal Collumpton Liberal with a gigantic spread on the table still waiting for the Party Leader.

By way of postscript Catherine told me that the pilot, trying to catch up time between Heathrow and Devon didn't climb to the normal cruising height but kept quite low which meant that they regularly hit air pockets. Apparently Keith felt sick the whole time, Catherine thought her last hour had come and Jo nonchalantly read the day's newspapers.

In comparison to today's fast moving, instant soundbite election campaigns, elections during Jo's leadership were slightly less high-tech but none the less gruelling. **Catherine Fisher**, Jo's right hand woman, did everything that is now done by an army of employees in Charles Kennedy's office.

I first went to work for Jo in 1953 for 6 months and I ended up staying for over 30 years. It was Jo's enjoyment of life and his never-ending sense of humour, which made it a pleasure to work for him. He worked at a tremendous speed. I remember on a Thursday, he used to come into the office before setting off for the weekend and ask, "Where am I going? What station do I go from?" and he would dash out of the office. I don't think he ever missed a train but there must have been a lot of near misses. I remember latterly, towards the end of his period as Leader, saying that he was getting too old to be nearly missing trains.

During the General Elections, Jo and I were on the move for the three-week campaign. After typing on my knee in the back of cars, planes and in hotel bedrooms it was a great relief to return to the Old Manse every now and then, when, with typical thoughtfulness, Laura would provide me with a large, firm table to work on - a luxury I still remember with gratitude.

Most residents of Orkney and Shetland over the age of 20 have clear memories of Jo and of Laura both during Elections or just going about their daily business. **John Scott** from Bressay in Shetland recalls the following images:

The vision of Jo collecting the female vote by wandering around Lerwick in a worn out raincoat.
Laura, one election when Jo was ill, bicycling round Bressay and memorably causing old Jimmy Smith - elder statesman of the Socialist Smith clan to take his eye off the road and tip his tractor into the ditch by the Bressay shop

In 1967, Jo decided that he had been Leader for long enough. In his memoirs he sums up his feelings at the time

"By 1967, I had been leader of the Liberal Party for 10 years. The Tory and Labour Parties go in and out of office. Few members of these parties keep the same job for more that 7 years at a stretch. No doubt to be a prominent member of these parties is more wearing but change breaks the monotony. For the Liberal Leader there is no such relief. I found myself staring at the same grey boards in the same Town halls. At General Elections, when politicians must repeat the same speeches

Hugh Crooks, editor of the Shetland Times, who was one of Jo's election team in Shetland, pictured walking through Lerwick in the 1960s (R Young).

over and over again, by the end of the campaign I would listen to myself in a detached way, silently commentating that we were about to have this passage or that. I now caught myself in the same trick even between elections. I found myself constantly striving to obtain something or other. It was time to be gone."

The weekend before Jo announced his retiral, **David Steel** was visiting Orkney to speak at a dinner organised by the Orkney Liberals. He recalls being asked into Jo's study for a chat just before they left for the function.

Jo pictured with David Steel and a group of Orkney Liberals at the Orkney Liberal Burns Supper just before he announced his retirement as leader.

Before we went out to the Dinner, Jo took me into his study and told me that I wasn't to go over the top in my speech as he was announcing to his colleagues the following week that he was resigning as Leader. You can imagine the shock this was for me. I had come into politics because of Jo. I was making my first visit as a young MP to the Leader's constituency and I had this important speech to make. Suddenly he dropped this bombshell on me before we went out and I wasn't allowed to say anything about it. In my book I record that I was completely shattered by this announcement and in his book, Jo records that I responded with Asquithian calm.

At that time election of Leader of the Liberal Party was decided on the votes of the Liberal MPs of whom there were 13. The candidates were Emlyn Hooson and Jeremy Thorpe. **James Davidson** who was then MP for West Aberdeenshire remembers that time

I was appalled by Jo's decision to stand down as leader of the party. He asked me if I would be prepared to stand for the leadership. I suspect he asked every one of his twelve disciples the same question! I explained my domestic situation and that I would not be defending my seat at the next General Election. "What about David Steel as leader?" I asked him. So far as I recall, Jo replied, "I think he's still a bit too young". In the event the leadership candidates were Emlyn Hooson QC, who had made his name in the Yorkshire Moors case, and Jeremy Thorpe. The choice rested with their fellow Liberal MPs. The evening before we were due to cast our votes, I was informed by Lobby correspondent, George Gardiner, later to become a Tory MP, that I was the only one of 13 who had not declared his intentions and that the score stood at 6 all. If George Gardiner was telling the truth, that gave me an unwelcome responsibility. I told him I had not yet decided. I suspected that both Jo Grimond and David Steel would be voting for Jeremy but I had not asked anybody. I spent a sleepless night. As a colleague, I preferred Emlyn Hooson who shared my interests in agriculture, foreign affairs and rugby football, but I was aware that he cut no ice on the floor of the House despite his experience as a barrister. Jeremy Thorpe on the other hand, had the ear of the House, including the Press Lobby and he was strongly supported by the Young Liberal movement – the future of the Party. With considerable misgivings, I gave Jeremy my vote. He won by 7 votes to 6.

Jo and Jeremy Thorpe walking along the beach during a Liberal Assembly.

JO AND LAURA

1967 - 1994

Jo became a backbencher again. This meant he had more time available to spend at home at the Old Manse in Orkney where he could indulge in his passion for his garden and ducks, the latter having the capacity to interrupt important calls from Downing St., as **Johnny Grimond** remembers:

My father was very fond of ducks. When he was asked by the BBC to do a radio programme called "Just Three Wishes", one of his wishes was for a duck pond (he also revealed that he would like, as God, to cure the world of poverty, and to be an artist).

The duck pond he described in the programme — a small, unpretentious affair no more than 20 feet across, in the middle of the lawn in front of the house — never came into being, but he had in fact built a duck pond in the garden some years before. The trouble was that the ducks for which it was intended never took to it. Like the old bath that it replaced, it had no running water and, though its sloping concrete sides were easier to negotiate than the slippery enamel of the bath, the ducks spurned it. My father turned it into a compost heap.

I think those ducks were the ones that my father was given at the farm of Lucknow in Shapinsay. We brought them home in a cardboard box, which my father set down in the kitchen as we came into the house: the telephone

Jo loved to potter in the garden when he was at home. (Phoenix Photos).

*was ringing, it was Downing Street on the line, and the Prime Minister wanted to
speak to my father about a matter of some urgency. Two minutes into the conversation
my father had to interrupt. There had been a breakout in the kitchen and, as he
explained to a surprised Ted Heath, "Four ducks have just entered the sitting-room
and I have to round them up. "Even without a proper duck pond, the Old Manse
garden, which is still largely as he left it, is a tribute to my father's determination
and energy. Working in it in all weathers, whether tying up roses, planting cabbages
or barrowing dung from Jimmy Brown's midden, he never gave up the struggle
against the elements. The trees around the house, many now 50 years old though
hardly huge, gave him special pleasure.*

Orkney Liberals at a Burns Supper in the Ayre Hotel in the late 1960s
Back Row L to R George Robertson, Robert Scott, John Fraser, William Muir, Edwin Eunson,
Frank Kent, Douglas Young, Norman King, Bobby Hutchison
Middle Row L to R Helen Taylor, Irene Scott, Nora Bremner, Dora Scott, Ann Harvey, John
Scott, Rognvald Harvey, Mary Hutchison, Netta Fraser, Eoin Scott, Jean Muir, Isabel Scott, Mrs
Slater, Margaret Eunson, Kate Partner, Mrs McLean, Mima Kent, Mrs King, Jimmy Bews,
Alan Thoms, Jenny Sinclair, Robert Learmonth, David Partner, Nessie Bichan, Jim Williams,
Mr McLean
Front Row L to R John Bremner, Maggie Scott, Grace Mowat, Mrs Robertson, Jeannie
Learmonth, George Mackie, Laura Grimond, Alex Doloughan, Elizabeth Thoms, Ruth Williams,
Kathy Hutchison.

In 1969, Jo stood for the Rectorship of Aberdeen University. His opponents included
disc jockey Jimmy Saville, satirist Willie Rushton, Clement Freud who was later
to become a Liberal MP and Robin Blackburn a former lecturer at LSE. Jo was
nominated by a coalition of the Liberal Society, the Celtic Society and the Shetland
Society. The final result put Jo in first place ahead of Robin Blackburn, with Clement
Freud in third place. (Dundee University later elected Freud as their Rector). **Robert
Brown** who is now an MSP was one of Jo's campaign managers.

I was Co - Chairman of the Grimond Rectorial Campaign along with Nigel Lindsay and Boyd Robertson and our campaign resulted in an epoch making victory over the other main candidate, Robin Blackburn who was supported by the Socialist Society. Jo attracted support from a wide range of people and after his election was the first to appoint a student, Kenneth Chew to be his Assessor.

I had the dubious pleasure of speaking for the Grimond Campaign at the Rectorial debate. I was terrified out of my wits having to speak to 1,500 students in the Mitchell Hall but in the end it didn't matter because no one could hear over the noise from competing factions.

THE PRESS AND JOURNAL   MONDAY DECEMBER 1 1969

RECTOR JO CELEBRATES WITH SUPPORTERS

Aberdeen University's new Rector, Mr Jo Grimond, M.P., enjoys a pint with some of his supporters at the Marischal Bar, Aberdeen, on Saturday evening.

Aberdeen University's new rector enjoying a pint with some of his supporters at the Marischal Bar, Aberdeen in November 1969 (Press & Journal).

Conrad Russell remembers that, years later in the House of Lords, Jo looked after the interests of Aberdeen and other Universities.

I remember in the House, in a period when financial stringency appeared to be about to lead to the closure of the University of Aberdeen I remember Jo pointing out to the Lord Chancellor that the Government could not close the University of Aberdeen without amending the Act of Union. I will always believe that it was that one act that saved the University. He was always a good and understanding friend of the Universities and capable of charming the birds out of the trees at six in the morning with an inimitably whimsical speech in defence of the humanities. For a moment, even in an exhausted House time seemed to have stopped.

Freed from the constraints of leadership, Jo also had more time to travel round the constituency and Mrs. **Margaret Anderson** from Shetland whom Jo had impressed as a schoolgirl in 1945 recalls meeting Jo again on one of his visits to Whalsay.

I met him again many years later, probably in the 70s when I was married with 5 children at home and my husband working on the island.
Milk has never been delivered on the doorstep in Whalsay. In the 70s it arrived in bottles three times weekly and was sold in the shop. Walking any distance carrying bottles of milk and messages was very tiring, although most families had cars by this time. I never learned to drive but on this occasion my husband and car were available to take me to the Hillhead Stores. I left my husband and children in the car and I went into the shop. There was Mr Grimond talking to the proprietor Mr.

Henry Stewart. I was heavily laden with two large baskets of messages, including many bottles of milk and I turned towards the door, Mr. Grimond turned round and took one of the baskets from my hand and asked if he could drive me home as he had a car outside. I almost said, "Yes please," then thought I would probably have to go home in the car with my husband. Mr. Grimond carried the heavy basket outside and placed it in our car. What a real gentleman.
I said to friends later I should have gone in Jo Grimond's car just to see the look on my husband's face as I ignored him and stepped into the car with our MP.

Jo at Symbister Pier, Whalsay during the 1970s.

While Jo was busy with politics, University business and looking after his constituency, Laura too, was active in the life of Orkney and Shetland and in politics in general.

Laura was renowned for her active mind but sometimes it meant that she was not paying full attention to the mundane aspects of everyday life. **Johnny** recalls one of his mother's more embarrassing moments.

Laura pictured at a picnic in Orkney.

My mother's head was never vacant; something was always going on there - usually it was politics: she had a view about everything she had heard on the news that day, and it was always a considered view, not a reflex response. Sometimes her thoughts were just occupied with the daily business of life: how to organise the next 24 hours. But, whatever she was doing, her mind was usually at work — and not necessarily on the matter in hand.

That, at any rate, seemed to explain the events that took place one morning in Orkney. My mother had been back from a shopping trip to Kirkwall for some time when I noticed a car parked at the back of the house. "Who's the visitor?" I asked, since I had seen none. 'What visitor?" she replied. "Well, whoever owns that car by the back door. " Then it became clear: that car was not her car. It was, in fact, a neighbour's, who had parked it innocently outside Spence's shop in Kirkwall while he went in to get a paper. Another car, my mother's (and also green), was there when he came out, but not his own. Alarmed at the growing incidence of theft in Orkney, he had gone to report his loss to the police. My mother, meanwhile, was driving merrily home to the Old Manse, untroubled by the unfamiliar features of the car plainly with her mind on other things. She later remarked that the radio had seemed a bit odd to her, since our car had none. Fortunately, neighbours are understanding in Orkney and charges were not pressed.

It was not only in Orkney that Laura could be a tad absent-minded. In London too she had her mind on other things. **Catherine Fisher**, Jo's secretary, remembers the following incident:

The story goes that Laura collected her mother's tiara from the bank. It was wrapped in brown paper and she placed it in the luggage rack on the bus. She got off the bus but forgot to pick up the parcel. No panic: she simply waited at the bus stop until the bus came round again, stepped onto the bus and collected the parcel from where she had left it.

With Jo no longer leader, Laura, who had always been active in the Women's Liberal movement, decided to try for a seat at Westminster. In 1968, **James Davidson** who was MP for West Aberdeenshire announced that, for family reasons, he would not fight the next General Election and Laura was selected as the Prospective Parliamentary Candidate.

MRS GRIMOND ADOPTED AT CULTS

Laura after being adopted as Liberal candidate for West Aberdeenshire, speaking at Cults academy in 1968. James Davidson, retiring MP on left, Jo on right (Press & Journal).

In 1968, I announced publicly that because of my wife's serious illness I would be standing down at the next General Election.
My intention was to give the West Aberdeenshire Constituency Liberal Association plenty of time to find another candidate. Unfortunately. It also gave the Tories the opportunity to ditch a no hope candidate and to trawl around for a high profile substitute. Eventually, they came up with Mad Mitch who had tossed a coin between the Nationalists and the Tories and had presumably lost. We invited Laura Grimond to stand for the Liberals.

This meant that there would be three Grimonds fighting seats, Laura in West Aberdeenshire, Jo in Orkney and Shetland and Johnny in North Angus and the Mearns.

David Eunson who had been a supporter of Jo's in Orkney was involved in Laura's campaign.

There was never much realistic prospect of three Grimond Members sitting in the House.
Johnny had a pretty hopeless task in North Angus and Mearns. He was up against a deservedly popular sitting Tory M.P. in Alick Buchanan-Smith, and when the result was declared he was last of the four candidates and lost his deposit.
Laura's position in West Aberdeenshire was quite different. It was a Liberal seat, having been captured in 1966 by James Davidson from Forbes Hendry, who had held it for the Conservatives.
James Davidson felt that for personal reasons he could not stand again, but the Liberals were very keen to hold on to the seat. Forbes Hendry did not try again, and the Conservatives adopted Lieut.Col. Colin Mitchell, better known as "Mad Mitch" West Aberdeenshire was an unusual constituency, large and heterogeneous. Much of it was rural; there were several small towns and villages: but an ever-increasing section consisted of suburban Aberdeen. Fast-growing communities on the outskirts of the city, like Dyce, Bridge of Don, and Cults, had closer affinities with the City constituencies than with places like Monymusk or Dunecht. The Member represented both Balmoral and Auchter Turra! This sociological mix made it a difficult seat to fight. In an obvious hit at the Liberal candidate Colonel Mitchell described it as a "man-sized" constituency.
He would not get away with that now!
Needless to say, Laura threw herself heart and soul into the campaign. She must have driven thousands of miles. Shortly before polling-day she noticed that her car-licence was months out-of-date. Fortunately she managed to put it right before anyone noticed! She spoke at innumerable meetings, and dealt with many questions. She was stumped once.
A retired minister asked a highly technical question about the teinds of quoad sacra parishes. Her reply was simple: "What's a quoad sacra parish?" In spite of that the minister promised her his vote. She also did a great deal of canvassing.
What sort of M.P. would she have been? It is an academic question, because the result gave Colonel Mitchell a majority of nearly six thousand, and she did not try again. She would have been very effective as a party spokeswoman, and no doubt as a Constituency Member also. She got on well with people. But the strain of having

two Members in the same family travelling such long distances would have been enormous.

Laura fought a very gallant and clean fight, and when it was all over there was no crying over spilt milk. She sat down and wrote personal letters to almost everyone involved. At a social gathering afterwards in Inverurie she cheered everybody up so much that they almost felt as if they had won!

Laura Grimond canvassing at an Inverurie factory when she stood for West Aberdeenshire in the General Election1970 (Stanley Devon).

Doreen Macpherson whose daughter Nora Radcliffe is now an MSP, was "cajoled" by Laura into being her agent in that campaign.

We in the West Aberdeenshire Liberal Association felt so privileged when Laura agreed to be our candidate in the 1970 Election. Apart from the political campaigning we shared with her we all had our lives enriched by the close contact and friendship of this great lady.

She was, in my experience, unique in lack of pretension. This allowed us, while in awe of her great intellect, organisational skill and incredible energy, to become close to her in friendship.

She was winning support everywhere she went but there was not enough time to cover such a wide constituency. It was not without trying and she became a familiar figure tearing around the country in her little mini. She took lodgings in Bucksburn, a suburb close to Dyce Airport, and her landlady, Mrs. Niven, was a blue-rinse, dyed in the wool Tory but like the rest of us she succumbed to Laura's charm and looked after her comfort fiercely in the face of Laura's self- neglect. By the time the election was drawing close Laura was having us working harder than we had ever thought possible and we were determined to give her all the support we could. Even so, I was taken aback one day when she told me I was to be her agent. I was terrified and tried to dodge what seemed to me a dreadful responsibility by saying that I lived in Culter - the campaign would be run from Inverurie – and I couldn't drive. I might have known better – within an hour or so she had the elderly retired manager of the Co-op in Culter organised to drive me to Inverurie each morning and a retired AA Patrolman in Inverurie to drive me home every night. That was it and because Laura had so much confidence in me, I believe I actually made quite a good job of it in the end!

Those were the days when a meeting was held in every town and village. We would cover much territory during the day, return to the Schoolhouse for a quick bite, and she would disappear to the bathroom for about 10 minutes and emerge with her short bobbed hair shampooed and bouncy and ready to take in at least 4 meetings looking as fresh as a daisy.

One afternoon doing Deeside, we found the Aboyne Gliding Club in session and before I knew what was happening my candidate was up among the clouds! We got good press cover about her getting a bird's-eye view of the Constituency.

It was a great joy to be with her at a mart and see how she could, with her impeccable accent, communicate with the Aberdeenshire farmers and win their, at first reluctant, respect and give and take repartee with great good humour on both sides.

It is odd little things that stay in your memory and I have a clear picture of her strolling through our garden and picking and eating blackcurrants straight from the bush! This must have impressed me as I need a lot of sugar to enjoy a blackcurrant tart. Another time she was staying with us over Hogmanay. My youngest daughter's birthday is the 1st of January and I was preparing for her party. I still don't know how it happened, but Laura and I brought in that New Year painting a lollipop tree on the wall of our kitchen – dining room and sticking on bright sweets in cellophane wrappings. Next day the kids didn't think it at all strange. My leaves were very much Primary 1 standard but all Laura's branches were very convincing. Looking through her obituaries the other day, I noticed that it mentioned in one that she "had a marked talent for painting".

My husband was a Scottish Nationalist and they never discussed politics but would regularly (and with sampling) discuss the relative merits of Bowmore, where he had been head teacher, and Highland Park.

I loved Jo from afar. It was admiration of him which brought me into the Liberal Party, but I loved Laura as a very dear friend who with so many demands on her

*time never forgot us in West Aberdeenshire
and until she suffered the stroke, always
kept in touch.*

James Davidson, the retiring MP, also
campaigned with Laura.

*When the Election came in 1970, I
accompanied Laura throughout her
campaign. Looking back, I think she
would have done better without me. In
marts, mills, schools, and public halls I
vehemently preached Liberal policy while
audiences waited patiently for Laura to
arrive. In the afternoon we canvassed
towns, villages and suburbs from
Balmedie on the coast, Bucksburn and
Cults on the outskirts of Aberdeen, to
Inverurie, Huntly and Braemar and the
headwaters of the Dee and the Don. On
the doorsteps, Laura was wonderful. Her
sincerity, humanity, and interest in people
shone through, but on the platforms or
rostrum her monotone West London voice
turned people off and gave them the
impression that she was a carpetbagger
from the south. The fact that she was the
wife of the highly respected and much
loved Jo Grimond counted for little. She
lost narrowly.*

*A great pity because she would have been
a great constituency MP and a champion
for equal opportunities for women.
Perhaps west Aberdeenshire's gain would
have been Orkney and Shetland's loss
because her organisational skills were of
great importance to the Liberals in the
Islands. The Grimonds were a great team.*

**Jo Grimond with characteristic purposeful
stride, at Grimsetter Airport, Kirkwall**
(**Harry Russell**).

In the 1970 election, Jo had his lowest majority ever. This was probably due to the fact that he was no longer leader of the party but also due to the fact that Laura was not in Orkney and Shetland to help coordinate the campaign. **Gelda Grimond** came north to help her father.

We missed my mother terribly. I don't know of anyone who brought more energy and fervour to political campaigning than my mother.

Magnus, Jo and Laura at home in the Old Manse of Firth in the early 1970s.

Fiona Cowan (née Scott) was a child in Westray during that election.

My first vivid memory of the Grimonds came after the General Election in 1970. During the election campaign a bundle of yellow posters arrived at our house in Westray for my Dad (Jack Scott) to distribute. This was no adventure for him but for me to be allowed paste and a brush was very exciting. Every telegraph pole in Aikerness soon proclaimed that we should " Vote for Jo the Man you Know". The next Saturday I persuaded Dad to drive me further afield and soon the entire Island was banana coloured with the message that "For Truth and Integrity Vote Jo". I never hear of integrity without thinking of Jo!

Jo boarding a small aircraft for a tour of Shetland in 1964 (Dennis Coutts).

Shortly after the election Jo phoned to thank my father for the help.
"That was all the bairns' doing " Dad said.
Imagine our surprise when' Jo later invited all the bairns of the Island to a thank
you party .
It was a big event in St George's Hall in Pierowall. (Now known as The Lodge and
run by Westray Buildings Preservation Trust) We all dressed up and were well fed
and entertained for the evening. Before the end we were all given a gift by Laura
- I got a green chiffon scarf! The other excitement was getting our pictures taken
by Johnny Grimond as we played Seat in the Bus.
What strikes me as unusual is that these days most politicians show interest in
children before elections - it was Jo's style to pay the compliment afterwards.

It can be difficult at the best of times to get to all parts of Orkney and Shetland but
during an election campaign when time is precious, it can prove almost impossible
to construct an itinerary round scheduled air and ferry services. Finding that he
would be unable to canvass North Ronaldsay, Jo approached Cllr. **Jack Scott** from
Westray who had his own aeroplane.

I got to know Jo very well over the years and as councillor for Westray and Papay,
it usually fell to me to chair his meetings at Election time. Jo was a regular visitor
to all the islands, but one election, he was having the usual difficulty in getting to
North Ronaldsay. I had a plane at that time and he asked if it was possible for me
to fly him there. I relished every excuse to fly and I was delighted to help Jo and have
his company during an interesting flight. I flew into Kirkwall to get him and was
a bit surprised to find that he intended to take Magnus with him. Now Magnus
looked as tall as his Dad and I had only got a peedie(small) plane. I was probably
going to be over the weight limit for take off. You can usually rely on the wind to
help in Orkney so nothing daunted, we took off for North Ronaldsay without incident
and the landing went well also. We taxied up to the 'terminal building' and Jo went
to his meeting. Jo then wanted to go to Papa Westray so we all climbed in and set
off. The wind was such that we had to get up speed as we climbed the hill. With the
added weight and the lightweight plane we were coming well up the field when I
wondered if we were going to take off. The dyke was rushing towards us and I
reckon we only cleared it by a few feet!

Magnus Grimond was 11 when his mother stood in West Aberdeenshire. He remembers what it was like to be a schoolboy with both parents involved in politics both local and national.

School in Orkney as the son of a public figure was testing at times. It was bad enough having one parent in politics, but having two might have been enough to break the camel's back.

Luckily from my point of view, my mother's adventure in national politics – she stood in the 1970 election in the West Aberdeenshire seat – was relatively short and unsuccessful. "Relatively unsuccessful" because she lost by a sufficiently narrow margin that I believe she might have won at the following election, when her rival, the former professional soldier Colin "Mad Mitch" Mitchell, bowed out of politics.

However, it was easy enough to take a detached view of these things when my mother was haranguing the electors of West Aberdeenshire. It was less comfortable for an adolescent schoolboy when, in 1974, she decided to stand for Orkney's new local authority, the Orkney Islands Council. And while she failed to persuade the West Aberdonians, the ratepayers of Firth and Harray proved more amenable to her blandishments, aided by the indefatigable Esther Laird.

By maintaining a "low profile", I avoided much of the caustic wit which schoolchildren reserve for their fellows, but there were times when her activities on the Council were too difficult for even me to avoid. One was the now infamous events surrounding the construction of the new public lavatories in Finstown.

When the brains in the Council Offices in School Place with, it has to be said, the reluctant support of the local councillor, decided that the advancing metropolis of Finstown would not be complete without a public urinal, few could have guessed at the splendour with which the new facility was to be fitted out. The fine Orkney stone walls and even finer flagstone roof was such a wondrous sight to behold it drew interest from as far away as Glasgow. Indeed, the Daily Record decided that Laura's Lavatory, as it was quickly christened, demanded a full-page spread. It is therefore perhaps fitting that my mother now looks out across this memorial to one of her finest achievements in her final resting-place in the old Finstown kirkyard.

"Laura's Loos" in Finstown (Ruth Williams).

Despite her prominence in such local cause célèbres as the saving of Papdale House, the South Isles ferries, the short-sea crossing and the building of the new Stromness Academy amongst many others, it was my father's job as M.P. which brought my most vivid memories of direct political activity in Orkney. I remember accompanying him around innumerable draughty parish halls at general elections and sometimes in between as well. The few hardy souls who ventured out were usually treated to a trenchant commentary on Britain's industrial decline and the failings of bureaucracies, whether in multi-national companies or, more usually, the civil service. The gravitas of these occasions was reduced somewhat by the metal chairs then popular in Orkney halls at that time, which invariably squeaked at key points during the speech as the occupants shifted to get closer to the hopelessly inadequate paraffin fire generally used to heat the room.

But general elections were great fun for a teenager, not so much for the cut and thrust of political debate or the clashing of great philosophies, but for the sticking up of posters. The objective was straightforward: to affix as many of your own to as many prominent locations as possible, while tearing down as many of the opposition's in the process. Road signs, walls and the road itself proved ideal bill boards. However, possibly the most audacious was the radiator grille of one prominent Tory's car. As I recall, the poster was attached to the front of the car with such skill that the owner drove around with it like a mobile sandwich board for the Liberal cause for several days before noticing.

Posters were, of course, not the only outlets for Orcadians' creative juices. For many years, travellers on the Kirkwall to Stromness road puzzled over an old lavatory strategically placed high on a bank near the Harray road end. The toilet lived on long after its purpose had been forgotten. Originally, in a reference to one of my father's most tenacious Tory foes, a sign above it had advertised it as "Firth's Seat". It was a publicity coup worthy of Saatchi & Saatchi.

However, graffiti has always brought out some of Orkney's finest political thought. There was the occasion, not this time at an election, when the then Secretary of State, Willie Ross, decided to visit the islands. A more hated figure it is hard to imagine. The Labour government, of which he was part, was in unusually bad odour with the farming community at the time and there was an only partly tongue in cheek campaign that Orkney go "back to Norway".

Such was the strength of feeling that the Secretary of State was burnt in effigy at the Stromness pier head. All along the route of his less than triumphant motorcade through the West Mainland he was met with signs of defiance, including the memorable "Free Orkney" daubed on the side of the Tormiston Mill in Stenness. But clearly the memory of the yoke of Westminster tyranny which Ross represented wore off fairly quickly, for not long afterwards some wag came along and added the word "butter" beneath the slogan, where it remained for many years.

Of course, my father could not have won and held Orkney and Shetland for so many years without an organisation unavailable to his adversaries. Stalwarts like Jeannie Learmonth, Alex Doloughan, Lib Shearer, Jack Twatt, Edwin Eunson, Jack Scott, Mr. and Mrs. Scott of Lyking, John Bremner of Bendigo and many others formed the backbone of the party, whether it was organising whist drives and jumble sales or getting the vote out at elections. But the M.P. also had an intelligence network second to none. Edward (Ned) Sinclair provided a unique historical perspective on the Liberal cause in Orkney. He also appeared to be able to pinpoint the political affiliations of half the Orkney electorate. Meanwhile, few Orkney events of any importance escaped the combined antennae of Helen Taylor, our housekeeper who looked after me for many years, and Jimmie Brown, our neighbour. Having subsequently been involved in many political campaigns further south, I remember Orkney elections with most affection. There was very little rancour or personal attacks. On the whole, everyone remained friends no matter which part of the political spectrum they occupied. The key ingredients were a sense of humour and not taking the whole thing too seriously – two things with which Orcadians are well supplied.

Johnny Grimond also remembers aspects of his mother's work as a councillor and campaigner:

Like my Father, my mother was a gardener too, but she left her mark on Orkney in other ways — sometimes in saving things that would have otherwise been destroyed. Long before conservation became an issue, for instance, she led the fight to prevent the demolition of Papdale House, Samuel Laing's birthplace in Kirkwall, and she also saved the Strynd from going the same way. She was instrumental in setting up the Hoy Trust and the Orkney Heritage Society.

Another of her acts on the council was to have a sign saying "Blind Summit" erected on a dangerous stretch of the old Kirkwall-to-Finstown road by Smerquoy. After a while, rather surprisingly, similar signs appeared on other Orkney roads. I'm not sure whether as many people associate her name with these signs as they do with the Finstown lavatories, but if so, I don't think she would mind. She had a sense of humour: in one of the general elections when the Tory candidate was John Firth of Rousay, it was she who arranged for all the signatures on my father's nomination papers to be those of other John Firths. And, though her mind was always occupied, she was above all a practical person, a doer.

Jo seated in the Orkney chair which was presented to him in 1975 to mark the 25th anniversary of his Election. L to R Lady Thurso, Lord Thurso, Jo, Magnus, Laura and Camilla Sinclair, daughter of Lord & Lady Thurso.

To this day there is no party politics in local elections in Orkney although, then as now, a number of councillors showed their "true colours" at General Elections. Laura stood as an Independent candidate. **Brenda Robertson** was an Orkney Islands Councillor for many years and she recalls Laura's impact on local politics

Laura and I served together when she joined the Council in 1974. She was the Chairman of the Housing Committee and I was Vice Chairman of the Social Work and Environmental Health. She was marvellous to work with - very active, and passionately keen to avoid extravagance.

In that year we were preparing to move from the County Council premises (the present Tourist Offices) to School Place. There were those who warmly welcomed the prospect of loads of posh new furniture – not however Laura, who felt that wherever possible, existing furniture should be used. One day, the two of us were inspecting the furniture in the old building and had discovered a table which Laura was convinced could be put to good use, with a little improvement. As time was of the essence, I felt we should be able to quote the actual measurements, and in the unfortunate absence of a measuring tape, Laura came up with an alternative solution. She said "'I'll lie down beside it on the ground - I'm 5'5" and you, Brenda, can measure with your hand the extra space between the top of my head and the chair legs ", which we did with Laura completely disregarding the state of the grubby floor which can have done her coat no good at all.

On another occasion, we were inspecting the public toilets in Stromness. Having looked over the "Ladies", in the North End, we approached the Pier Head, where Laura spotted the ancient "Gents" loo - and watched with interest by the Pier Head Parliament, headed straight for it. I hung back, musing it would be inappropriate for us to enter; but fortunately, the accompanying Environmental Health Officer~ acting quickly, leapt in front of her and bellowed a strangulated warning. Just in time - a red-faced local youth shot out, much to the enjoyment of the spectators. Laura was not one whit abashed.

Things were never quite the same after Laura left the Council.

Life was not all work, Jo, Laura and Magnus went on a private visit to the Faeroe Islands but their fame had gone before them as **Sofus Poulsen**, the Faroese Commercial Attaché at the Royal Danish Embassy recalls:

In 1972, my wife and I were in Torshavn for the Nordic Fisheries Conference when we met Mr. and Mrs. Grimond and their barely teenage son who had arrived on a private visit to our islands. Needless to say when our Prime Minister and Government were told that Jo Grimond MP for Orkney and Shetland and his family were visiting our islands, they speedily arranged a luncheon in his honour at the Hotel Foroyar attended by many of our eminent public personalities. I remember Jo saying that he was most impressed at the welcome and hospitality afforded to him and his family especially as he was on a private visit. Another special event which took place during the same week was a Gala Dinner given by the Government with over 500 people present. I recall meeting Jo at the entrance when he arrived for dinner and he mentioned that although Faeroe was officially a dry country, he had never seen so much drink in all his life.

It is expected of the Member of Parliament that he should be available to see his constituents should they visit London. It might be thought that with one's constituents many hundreds of miles away that this would not happen often to the Member for Orkney and Shetland, but Orcadians and Shetlanders have always had a taste for travel and there are many people who remember Jo's tours of the House and subsequent refreshments. **John Scott** from Bressay in Shetland remembers a family visit to the House of Commons in the 1970s.

My memory is of a bucolic Jo - an hour late for lunch with the Nigerian High Commissioner - taking the Scott family (Tavish who was 11 and Kirsty 9) on his tour of the Houses of Parliament. The esteem and affection of the permanent staff for Jo was the lingering memory, even to the Commons bar with ginger beer for the children.

The event must have made an impression on Tavish, as he is now the MSP for Shetland.

Laura Grimond's visit in March 1985 to Hastings & Rye Women's Liberal Association. She is pictured with the WLA Councillors on Hastings Borough Council and the President of Hastings WLA.. L to R Cllr Jane Amstrad, Cllr Pamela Brown. Cllr Mollie Trowswell, Cllr Marguerite Itall, and seated Doris Taylor Smith (President) and Lady Grimond.

Laura was very active in the Women's Liberal Association in the 70s and 80s. She addressed conferences and attended functions all over the UK. For many she was an inspiration and for others she was a friend who could be relied on to help promote the Womens' Liberal Movement.

Cllr. **Jean Glynn** remembers attending a function at which Laura was present:

Apart from all her splendid intellectual qualities, Mrs. Grimond was also very charming and friendly. Many years back I attended a function at the National

Liberal Club at which Laura Grimond was the chief guest. My own surname is rather similar to hers and another guest to whom I was introduced mistook me for Laura Grimond so that a very odd conversation ensued.

Later in the evening, I myself was introduced to the real Laura Grimond and I related the incident to her and added that I had been extremely flattered to have been mistaken for her. Back came the immediate and very gracious reply, " Oh no, it is I who should be flattered, You are so much younger and better looking than I am!!" You can imagine how cheering and pleasing this was to a young member.

Laura Grimond speaking at Castle Howard, Yorkshire. Dame Christian Howard, Lady Sear, Elizabeth Shields, MP and Christina Barron, chairman of the Women's Liberals at the Centenary of the Women's Liberal Federation in June 1986.

Laura was a frequent visitor to Yorkshire Liberal functions and **Joyce Wainwright** recalls a misprint from the local newsletter.

Laura was very interested in alternative systems to the "rates" and one of her speaking engagements was billed in the local newsletter as "Rapes – What are the alternatives?" - Speech by Laura Grimond.

Laura Grimond speaking on "What are the Alternatives to Rates?" in Huddersfield in March 1986 with Kathleen Hasler, Cllr David Shutt, Cllr. Heather Swift, chaired by Joyce Wainright and organised by the Yorkshire Women's Liberals.

Laura was never one to avoid the difficult issues of politics. During the 1970s Laura went to Belfast to find out for herself the effects of the Troubles on the women of Belfast. **Ronald Farr** of the Ulster Liberal Party recalls the visit:

She met us in Belfast at the height of the troubles and got Sheelagh Murnaghan to arrange for her to spend a night in an ordinary house in Ballymurphy, one of the major housing estates in West Belfast. Unlike many politicians she did not seek publicity offering instant -solutions but she showed genuine interest and concern. I wrote in my diary on Monday 24 January 1972 about the dinner Mrs. Grimond had in the Wellington Park Hotel, Belfast with the Ulster Liberal Party executive including Sheelagh, Rev Albert McElroy, president, John Quinn chairman and myself secretary: "Mrs. Grimond as charming and intelligent as expected. Just up from University College Dublin where she with Jo, Lord Caradon and Liam Cosgrave were pelted with eggs and tomatoes by Republicans. Wide-ranging conversation on local situation Orkney, Shetland, Faroes, Rhodesia, cost of living etc. Mrs. G. insisted on giving £2 to ULP funds. "
It was a great privilege to have met both Grimonds and I am sure they will long be remembered with great affection.

1974 saw two Elections one in February and one in October and at both Jo was returned to Westminster with his majority back to a respectable level. His SNP opponent in the October Election was **Howie Firth** who was later to become the chief producer for Radio Orkney.

An election campaign in Orkney and Shetland is particularly gruelling as every parish, every island and every village has to be visited and the skill of the election organiser is to try and get one two or even three islands covered in one day. Often the candidates hardly see each other until they meet at the count. At the end of the campaign I had the utmost respect for Jo – not only had he fought that kind of campaign on several occasions before, but he had simultaneously built up support for the Liberals nationally and lead national campaigns while at the same time keeping up the quality of National debate.

In 1976 Jeremy Thorpe resigned and Jo was urged by many in the Party to take over the leadership again until the next General Election. Jo was unwilling to do this but agreed to take over as interim leader until the one member one vote election decided whether the new leader should be John Pardoe or **David Steel** who recalls an incident from that time.

During the confusing period after Jeremy Thorpe had resigned, we decided that Jo should become temporary leader while the Party underwent constitutional changes

Jo at home in the Old Manse of Firth in the 1970s.

to enable the leader to be elected by the membership. This required a full-blown special Party Conference. The Party general secretary reported difficulty in obtaining a venue at such short notice and said it might have to be Bellevue Zoo in Manchester! "We can't possibly go there", I opined testily, "we would be a laughing stock." "On the contrary", Jo replied wearily, " I can think of no more appropriate location for such an event. "

In order to fight elections, money has to be raised and the Annual Liberal Sale.......one in Orkney and one in Shetland were the main fundraising events and largely overseen by the ladies from the Women's Liberal Associations under Laura's direction. **Ruth Williams** has helped at Liberal Sales since the 1960s

There was a large raffle, for which tickets were sold for weeks beforehand in every parish and small shop on the islands, a small "cloakroom ticket" raffle numerous sales tables with homebakes and handicrafts not to mention white elephant stall and tea with more home bakes. The morning would be spent setting out the stalls and the Community Centre was always a hive of activity and Laura was always at the centre of things...not just telling people what to do but doing it herself. It was a great draw if another MP would come to open the Sale, as this would guarantee a large attendance. In Orkney, the Sale would be followed by a Grand Rainbow Whist in the evening where the prizes were large tins of fruit salad.... I think this dated from the 1950s when things were still rationed. A great deal of money would be made and this meant that both Constituency Associations always had sufficient funds to fight the elections.

Jim Wallace, Laura and Charles Kennedy at the produce stall at the Orkney Liberal Sale 1987 (Charles Tait).

Laura also coordinated the Shetland Liberal Sale with helpers such as Jim and **Margaret Crossan** who recalls:

Every year Laura used to help organise the Liberal Sale in Shetland. She was not afraid to ask anyone to contribute and everyone did. She would go around Lerwick cajoling goods from shopkeepers for the raffle and then with my husband, Jim, would set off complete with picnic lunch to Nesting and Vidlin where they collected things to sell and persuaded people to buy raffle tickets. The car would come back laden with eggs, baking and knitting.
Laura was completely at ease with whoever she met, be it an old lady in a Shetland croft or someone thought to be important. She treated them all the same.

Jim Crossan, Laura, Rosie, Helen and Jim Wallace outside the Town Hall, Lerwick in April 1987.

Not only were MPs in demand to open the Sale, they were also a draw for a Dinner. **Sir Cyril Smith** came to Orkney to attend such a dinner in the 1970s.

I recall with great joy, the week that my late mother and I spent with Jo and Laura Grimond at their home in Orkney.

At that time Jo was the temporary Party Leader yet when I went with him to address meetings on the Island, he said he had to go early to put out the chairs! So humble - yet so great.

Shopkeepers told me that Laura "expected" them to donate prizes annually to the Liberal Sale.

When I was Chief Whip of the Party, Jo used to come and see me each week to inquire what the votes were for the next week. Jo did not relish three line whips and neither did I - and when there was one - he'd reply "Well I'll try to be there but I can't promise" - yet I never remember him missing one!

Jo commanded respect without compulsion.

Jo did not like being forced to stay in the House of Commons for a vote. **Alan Beith** recalls a story told by the late David Penhaligon about the last days of the Callaghan Government in the late 70s when there were a lot of late votes with three line whips attached.

By that time Jo did not relish late votes and he was unwilling to stay for one particularly late vote because the last Tube would have gone. "Why don't you get a taxi home ?" someone enquired. Jo indicated that that was far too extravagant a solution. "OK" said David Penhaligon, putting a coin on the table, "we'll all give you 50p towards your taxi fare." All those present also put 50p on the table. Jo pocketed the money and stayed for the vote

Even towards the end of his parliamentary career, Jo made a huge impression on those who met him. **J.A. Stephen** remembers being impressed at how Jo was willing to talk to him as a new member of the Party.

Many years ago I attended a Liberal Conference at Llandudno. I was new to the Party and very inexperienced and naturally I very much respected and looked up to our elder statesman , Jo Grimond. What a pleasure it was to fall into step with Jo on the way to the conference that sunny morning. I had grown up used to a two-tier society and yet here I was chatting away to the ex leader of our Party on a one to one basis. Nothing convinced me more that I had made the right choice in joining the Liberals - truly a 'One Nation Party'.

Later I read his memoirs and got to know and like this gentleman who through great personal effort and courage led our Party, with such style. Oh for more genuine, caring politicians such as Jo in Westminster today!

His influence on my life has been very strong. It was he who made me realise that there is no limit to what we can achieve. Above all he gave me confidence, I now run my own Postal Stamp business and am also Chairman of Wyre Forest Constituency Association. How sad that Jo was not able to see the dawning of the new age that is our inheritance for the efforts of men like Jo .

As well as charming the individual, Jo was still able to charm an audience. Just before the 1979 Election, **David Alton** was the Liberal candidate in the Liverpool Edge Hill by-election

I was fighting the by-election in 1979 in Edge Hill where Jo's friend Major Irvine had been MP. Jo came to speak as warm up act for David Steel and stole the show. His sense of mischief lead him to say some nice things about the rookie candidate but worryingly he added, "…there was one thing with which I profoundly disagreed. Mr Alton said that we are not better people than our opponents, just that our way of doing things was a better way. It isn't true. We are better people." He ended by introducing David Steel and said that he realised that the only reason he had been asked was to get an audience for David Steel. Needless-to-say, his Liverpool audience loved every irreverent moment.

Jo "Gets on his bike" outside the Members' Entrance at the Palace of Westminster.

Jo at Baltasound Post Office, Unst during campaigning in the 1979 General Election.

Paddy Ashdown remembers the help Jo gave him as a PPC in the 1970s.

I remember as a new aspiring PPC in Yeovil (then very far from being recognised as a winnable seat), when, in the late 1970s, he came to Yeovil to talk about workers co-operatives to Westland workers. He electrified them and put me on the map in my Constituency. More than any other thing, this event was what set me and the local Party on the road which eventually ended up with us winning the seat.

Later, when I was Party Leader he gave me similar support in the dire early days of the Party after its formation and was from the very start of my period of Leadership, the Leader of our Party I most tried to emulate.

None of which is to ignore the human things that made him such good company and such a good friend. His Scottish carefulness with money. His dry wit and his capacity for endearing and unexpected quirkiness. But above all his capacity to spellbind in private quite as much as he could a public audience. Liberals should not have heroes, because, to believe in heroes, you also have to be believe in dwarfs. Nevertheless, each of us has someone whose light we seek to follow and whose actions we try to emulate. Like so many of my generation Jo was my early pontifical inspiration - the person who made me understand I was a Liberal.

We are not over supplied with politicians about whom you could use the word "great" in politics today. But for me, Jo was undoubtedly one.

Jo speaking in Kirkwall during the 1979 General Election (Charles Tait).

The 1979 election was the last one which Jo fought. This time he had a majority of 6810. He was 66 and becoming increasingly deaf. This meant everyday conversation was a trial and other aspects of the job as MP became more difficult. He decided mid-term that he would not stand at the next election and the hunt was on for a successor. There was speculation that Gelda, Johnny or Magnus might come forward but no. In a letter to his friend Charles Keen, Jo wrote:

Dear Chas,

V. kind of you to write - greatly appreciated. Perhaps its time to stop when some people think you might go on. Soon after I first got into the House Of Commons someone stopped me in the Lobby and said," Jo, Why didn't you speak in that debate? - and an old buffer who overheard it remarked. "Never mind when people ask why you didn't speak my boy – look out when they ask why you did!"
Mag will not come forward nor has Gelda - who is the real politician in the family.
Yours Jo

Jo took no part in the search for his successor but Laura was in her element and in March 1983, a 28 year-old advocate called **Jim Wallace** was selected to be the next candidate for the Orkney and Shetland seat. Jim recalls

I didn't meet Jo until after I had been selected as the candidate. He was always supportive but let me make my own way, both in the build up to the election and once I became MP. Shortly after I was elected, the thorny issue of seal culling came to the fore. I was receiving numerous letters from those on both sides of the argument and as seal culls had been carried out during Jo's tenure, I went to ask him how he had dealt with the issue.
"I went on holiday" was the reply.

Jo Grimond in Albert Street during the 1979 General Election (Charles Tait).

Liberal PPC Jim Wallace with Jo on the Cornslip, Kirkwall prior to the 1983 Election (Charles Tait).

Jim was then engaged to **Rosie Fraser** who recalls her initial visits to Orkney and her impressions of Jo and Laura.

I first met Laura and Jo when Jim was selected as the prospective candidate in March 1983. I was new to the whole business of politics and only had childhood memories of Jo from news bulletins and TV programmes. I was very overawed by meeting and staying with the Grimonds.

It was likely that an election was imminent and it was hoped to be able to hold the Orkney Liberal Sale before the campaign started, so it was agreed that I would fly to Orkney on the Friday, help Laura with the Sale preparations while Jim went to Shetland. David Steel was to fly into Shetland on the Saturday morning in his leader's private plane; campaign with Jim and both would arrive in Orkney on Saturday at lunchtime to attend the Sale. So for 24 hours I was on my own without Jim.

Shortly after I arrived in Orkney so did the fog. Laura and I drove very briskly round the West Mainland in the thickest fog imaginable. I soon learned that every time I spoke to Laura, she turned her head in my direction in order to reply, thus taking her eyes completely off the road. The more she talked to me, the more I looked straight ahead into the thick mist ready to shout "cow" or "tractor" or whatever hazard might be looming towards us.

We awoke the next morning to find that the fog had gone.......to Shetland. Laura, dressed in her floral apron and armed with the produce we had collected the day before disappeared into Kirkwall in the car to set up the tables for the afternoon event, leaving me at the Old Manse with Jo. At about 10.30am, the phone rang ....and rang. Jo who was somewhere in the house seemed totally oblivious to the insistent ringing and it was a while before I realise that because of his deafness, he hadn't heard. Having told him the phone was ringing, he answered it and it transpired it was David Steel...at Kirkwall Airport....two hours early because Shetland was fogbound. Jo promised to come to the airport forthwith to pick him up and put the phone down. There was only one drawback to this plan. Laura had the car. When this was pointed out to Jo, he just said "I'm sure she'll be back soon." and went on with what he had been doing before the phone call. It was over an hour later when Laura returned. Neither of them seemed particularly worried that David had been sitting at Kirkwall Airport for over an hour, expecting to be picked up at any moment, and David did not seem surprised that it had taken us so long to come and get him. He knew Jo much better than I did.

I then went to have lunch with Jo and David Steel and John Bremner the constituency chairman and I remember being totally out of my depth as I attempted to make conversation. David Steel then deputised for Jim and opened the Sale.......perhaps the first time a leader has deputised for a mere candidate.

On the Sunday we went to church and I sat between Jo and Laura. When the minister, who I learned later from Jo was renowned for preaching long sermons, had been in full flow for about 15 minutes, Jo started to drum his fingers noisily on the pew while he studied the ceiling. Thinking that Jo, with his hearing loss, did not realise the noise he was making, I expected Laura to lean over and indicate that he should be quiet but Laura seemed totally engrossed in studying her hymn book and paid no attention. The drumming continued and after about thirty seconds, the minister's preaching seemed to falter and in another minute we were onto the next part of the service. I was most impressed both at the power of an MP over the clergy and at their openness and hospitality towards me.

The Election was called on the Monday following that weekend and on the dissolution of Parliament, Jo ceased to be MP for Orkney and Shetland, a position he had held for 33 years.

During the Election which followed, Laura was **Jim Wallace's** agent as Jim remembers

Pictured following lunch in the Kirkwall Hotel prior to the 1983 Liberal Sale are Rosie Fraser (Wallace), David Steel, Jo Grimond, Nora Bremner and John Bremner (Phoenix Photos).

It was tremendous having Laura as my agent because she knew Orkney and Shetland so well. I remember in the first week, she sent me to the North Isles of Orkney. I wasn't sure where I was going or what I was supposed to do when I got there but there were people to meet me who took me round. Laura's strategic thinking was that if you made a good enough impression the residents of the North Isles then word would get back to all their relatives in Kirkwall. This was much easier than knocking on all the doors in Kirkwall. I remember going with Laura to the Balfour Hospital ostensibly to visit someone whom she knew had been discharged the day before but she had reckoned quite rightly that once in the ward she would spot someone she knew and from there we could "work" the whole ward, which we did. Laura thought that the campaign should end with a piece of razzmatazz and she organised an eve of poll car cavalcade through Kirkwall. This involved Rosie and myself standing on the back of a Landover pick-up waving while we were driven around Kirkwall with about 10 cars covered in posters and tooting their horns behind us and someone on a loudspeaker exhorting everyone to "Remember to Vote. Vote Liberal – Vote Wallace" With great confidence Laura led us into a

Kirkwall housing estate and into a dead end. The whole cavalcade had to do three point turns to the extreme delight of hordes of children who had been following us. However most of those of voting age were ensconced in their living rooms and did not witness this, so I was duly elected as the MP two days later.

I will always be eternally grateful to Laura for the encouragement, support and utter dedication with which she threw herself into the campaign as my agent because without her, I would not be in the position I am today.

Jim Wallace with Liberal supporters outside the OIC offices after his election victory. Back row, L. to R. - Brian Sutherland, Andy Hajducki, John Bremner, Jim Wallace, Rosie Fraser (Wallace), Ruth Williams, Arthur Irvine, Alistair Easton. Front row Sandy Aldie, Catherine Hajducki, Kenneth Hajducki, Jamie McLeod, Gayle Hajducki and Laura Grimond.

Alistair Easton was a friend of Jim's from his days at Cambridge and was one of the campaign workers in Shetland. He remembers that Laura liked to start the day early.

During the 1983 Election, Jim frequently stayed with me when he was in Shetland, and I therefore became the recipient of the Early Morning Phone Calls from Laura. Laura must have been an early riser, and must have been at her most inspired in the early morning. Day after day I dragged myself from bed at 7.00 am to answer the phone and speak to a very wide-awake Laura with her latest ideas on what "Jim must do". At this distance, I cannot remember any specifics, but I remember that many of the ideas showed that Laura was letting her endless enthusiasm run away. I do remember that, while Jim did sometimes follow her instructions, most were rejected and quietly forgotten about, safe in the knowledge that, by lunchtime, Laura would have had so many new ideas that those of the early morning had been forgotten about.

The campaign also gave me the opportunity to study Laura on the campaign trail. One Saturday night, Jim, Laura and I arrived at the Olnafirth Primary School for Jim's 8.30 election meeting, the third of the night. Not exactly to our surprise, we found the people of Voe had better things to do as no one arrived for the meeting. We therefore decided to go and find the voters and headed for the Norseman's Inn at Weisdale. Laura headed purposefully for the Public Bar and, half pint of lager in hand, worked the room like the real pro she was. It might be thought that a relatively elderly lady from her background would not fit in well in the twenty something clientele, but far from it. Her memory for names meant that, as soon as she heard someone's name, she could remember something about their parents or grandparents and she charmed her way round the room. The ultimate line was however reserved for two construction workers from the central belt, working at Sullom Voe. When told by them that they were not locals, coming instead from Paisley, without a pause she replied, "Paisley, my Grandfather was MP for Paisley." Only Laura could have such style.

Ruth Williams who had helped in many of Jo's Election campaigns remembers Laura's desire that every possible vote should be secured.

Laura was very keen that as many of those who were entitled to vote should cast that vote. This was not purely a high-minded principle. She said that as the Liberals usually got around 50% of the vote, if four people were encouraged to vote, then two would vote Liberal and the votes of the other two would be split amongst the opposition. Laura was therefore very keen to make sure that all those voters who were temporarily or permanently incapacitated received a postal vote. In the 1983 Election, with the deadline for postal vote applications looming, she needed the signature of the local surgeon on the application form. He happened to be on the golf course at the point furthest from the Clubhouse. Not to be outdone, Laura set off across the golf course with me trailing in her wake to find Peter Konstam. Having secured the signature, Laura borrowed a ball and club from poor Peter and played "pitch and putt" all the way back to the Clubhouse.

Laura's efforts as agent made sure that Jim Wallace was elected with a handsome majority….not quite as good as most of Jc's but respectable and thus lived up to the slogan of the campaign

THE LIBERAL FLAME MUST NEVER DIM…
PASS IT ON FROM JO TO JIM.

Orkney Liberals at a dance in Firth to mark Jo's retiral and Jim Wallace's election. Back row, L. to R. Nora Bremner, John Bremner, Kathy Hutchison, Jo, Jim Wallace, Ruth Williams, Kim Gee, Diana Troup, Edwin Eunson, Jim Troup. Front row, Laura, Rosie Wallace, Margaret Eunson.

Jo received a life peerage and took the title Lord Grimond of Firth. Laura did not like being Lady Grimond….she felt that if the peerage had been hers, Jo would still have been called Mr. Grimond and she saw no reason why she should be a "Lady" In Orkney and Shetland most people still referred to them as Mr. and Mrs. Grimond or just Jo and Laura. **Margaret Crossan** wrote the following poem in Shetland dialect and she read it at Jo's retirement party in Shetland,

Fir mony lang years he has stood fir wis,
And spoken on wir behalf.
Ita da Hoose o Commons an der dey say,
He pat Shetlan' on da map.

We hae ta tank him for mony things,
Dat he has done fir wis,
Bit maest o aa whit we laek best,
Is his happy weel kyent face.

He most be tired o travaillin,
Steppin on and aff o planes.
I bet he's blyde dat noo he can,
Spend more o his time at hame.

Lord Grimond O' Firth dey caa him,
Wir pleased hit sood be so,
Bit here i'da isles whaar we luv him,
He'll aye be kent as Jo

Jim and Margaret Crossan with Jo at his retiral function in Shetland.

In 1987 Jo and Laura were given the Freedom of Orkney. It was perhaps fitting that the Convener of the Orkney Islands Council who bestowed the honour was none other than Edwin Eunson who had been one of Jo's most loyal supporters since 1950.

Jo and Laura were made Freemen of Orkney in August 1987 (Charles Tait).

Jo still attended the House of Lords regularly and fulfilled speaking engagements. **Monroe Palmer** remembers Jo speaking at a meeting in the late 80s.

Jo's public appearances got rarer as his hearing became a problem for him However, we were once lucky in the London Borough of Barnet in the late 80s to entice him to a public meeting in Finchley. The speakers were an SDP MP and Jo. I asked to take the Chair. My preference for a Chair of a meeting is that he/she says as little as possible. So I introduced the first speaker and then Jo (a much older man than the hero of my youth). He spoke and I felt the adrenaline flowing. Jo finished and resumed his seat. Without thinking I rose and my words displayed all my inner enthusiasm roused by Jo's speech. Behind me I heard the voice of one of the platform party, " Monroe's off again", but I couldn't stop. I had to impart my excitement to the audience.

Laura was also terrific. A person whose opinions I sought over the years and who was always happy to advise a green PPC.

Jo's sense of humour was never far from the surface and his wit meant that all who heard him speak were greatly amused even if he did not always stay on the subject in hand **Rosemary Pettit** recalls hearing him speak in the 80s.

I have one anecdote, which seems to me typical of Jo Grimond's freewheeling spirit In the mid-eighties I attended a reception at the London Book Fair hosted by the Scottish Publishers Association and at which Jo Grimond had been invited as the guest speaker.
After the usual canapés and introductory remarks, Jo got up to speak. He set off with brio and at a good pace although none of us knew where he was going and very few of his remarks had anything to do with publishing. Eventually his thoughts gathered round the subject of Scottish devolution and focused on the earlier referendum.
Then he pronounced, 'The reason why the Scots - when it actually came to it did not vote for devolution was that they feared being ruled by the English less than they feared being ruled by Glasgow trades unionists and Edinburgh lawyers!'

Jim, Jo and Edwin Eunson at a function in the Commodore Motel in May 1990 to celebrate 40 years of Liberal representation in Orkney (Charles Tait).

Speeches were not all light-hearted affairs. He still had the ability to use political oratory and this he did in the eighties to promote the Alliance **Lord Rodgers** remembers Jo turning up to help Roy Jenkins.

I have an almost visual memory of Jo in Warrington when he turned up to support Roy Jenkins in the SDP's first by-election. He arrived without warning, came into the Committee Room, and asked whether there was anything he could do. Soon he was out in the gloomy streets, looking slightly lost in our noisy electioneering, rather diffidently approaching voters but doing the world of good to our whole Alliance team. It was a symbolic gesture from a man whom I had come greatly to respect.

By the early 90s Jo was quite a lot frailer but still attending the House of Lords. In 1992 Laura seemed as active as ever and was very concerned about the plight of Bosnian refugees and was actively working out how some might be accommodated in Orkney. It was a great shock to all when she suffered a debilitating stroke in February 1992. After a period in hospital in Orkney she went south for intensive rehabilitation and with her usual determination and vigour she made a remarkable recovery but she was much frailer and was left with speech difficulties......a very frustrating state for someone such as Laura to whom communicating with people had been her existence. She returned to stay at the Old Manse with Jo caring for her. In October 1993, Jo too suffered a stroke but he did not survive and he died on 24th October. Laura was quite lost without him and it was only a few months later in February 1994 that she too, died.

Their friends from Orkney, Shetland and the wider world of politics attended their funeral services in St Magnus Cathedral and their joint memorial service in London. They are both buried in their adoptive Orkney in the kirkyard in Finstown.

Jo and Laura at home in the 1970s.

TRIBUTES

We have decided to publish in full some of the tributes made at the time of their deaths, at Jo and Laura's respective funeral services and at their joint Memorial Service. We feel these sum up the lives of two remarkable people who are remembered and missed by all those who met them.

Memories Of Jo Grimond

By Howie Firth
(This was broadcast on the news of Lord Grimond's death.)

To a whole generation of us, Jo Grimond was as integral a part of Orkney as Skara Brae or St Magnus Cathedral. He became a national figure by sheer flair, with the kind of natural elegance that you only find in the true masters of their field. It's the assurance of the cricketer who stands at the crease and casually flicks the fast bowler to the boundary. In the north, where the winters are long and dark and made for reading books, intellectual skill is prized, and in conciseness of thought and clearness of vision, Jo Grimond shone.

I remember recording a radio interview with him in the 1987 election, when he was well into retirement, but clearly delighted to have an opportunity to float ideas. Did he think, I asked him, that the Tories under Mrs Thatcher had become the new radicals? His reply, sparkling and incisive, would grace any political manifesto of the present time.

When I stood against him in the 1974 General Election, I didn't realise at the time how it would produce a kind of bond. Jo had the professional's eye in politics, and anyone who had become involved had joined the club, ... particularly if they were there to share ideas. Interviewing him subsequently for radio became something like turning the pages of a friend's photograph album. He would talk about the great political hecklers of Orkney and Shetland, from the days before television when political meetings were glorious confrontations of marvellous repartee; he would recall the epic journeys around the constituency in election campaigns where every island must be visited, by small boat or aeroplane. In the early days after the war, the candidates had often to travel around together on the steamer, and would land at various island piers to speak to the assembled populace, one by one.

One of Jo's strongest Orkney supporters was a man who divided the world into two categories - Tories, who were 'rank'; and Liberals, who were 'staunch.' Jo as a man, and as representative of the Party which when in government had brought in the crofting legislation, inspired such support. And he was a staunch friend of the isles; as one of his lifelong Shetland friends well put it, when the chips were down, you knew you could rely on him. In the late sixties, for example, he fought tirelessly, courageously and articulately to keep the island authorities of Orkney and Shetland from absorption into the new super-regions of mainland Scotland. In the seventies, he steered through Parliament the legislation that gave Orkney and Shetland unique powers to control oil development for community benefit. I can remember the former Shetland Chief Executive, Ian Clark, describing the skill with which Jo would take from him highly complex and detailed documents, often with only a matter of minutes left before facing a Commons Committee, and identify the key points to highlight or beware.

He was an unusual politician because he had a long-term vision that covered all of society, combined with a warm humour and immense personal charm. He looked like a leader, in a way like an aristocrat from another age, and yet he appealed to the ordinary person because he spoke not with slogans, but with logic and clarity. He respected his audience's intellect, and invited them to join him in his analysis of political ideas. It was appropriate that someone who looked so much like a Prime Minister should marry the grand-daughter of Mr Asquith, and a brilliant political thinker and activist in her own right. In his talents, Jo Grimond harked back to a past age of greatness, but in his thinking he charted a course for the future. It really is this evening as if a light has gone out in the north, and a time for many memories.
BBC Radio Scotland, October 25th 1993

Tribute to Jo at his Funeral October 1993

By Jackie Robertson, Jo's agent in Orkney 1950 -70

I was highly honoured when I was asked to speak about my personal association with Jo Grimond extending to almost half a century. It began in 1950 when he stood again for election after a "near miss" in 1945. I was approached by a local Party member - my former school rector - and asked whether I was prepared to become Mr. Grimond's election agent.

I did not know Jo then but I accepted the job as a challenge. A few days later a tall handsome figure called at my office, stooping slightly as he entered my room door and modestly announced "I'm Grimond". Thus began a pleasant and enlightening association.

There followed a busy campaign with its hub in a room in Kirkwall with a band of dedicated and enthusiastic party workers presided over by Edwin Eunson who was virtually Jo's right-hand man, all orchestrated by Laura who was tireless in over seeing that all was progressing satisfactorily.

We planned a campaign of meetings and posters. My suggestion of "Vote for Jo the man you know" was agreed and duly exhibited. The Tory opposition immediately displayed a

counter - "Don't fiddle, "Banjo". However their instrument was out of tune with the electorate. There followed meetings throughout the County - in each town, parish and island planned to fit in with Jo's frequent visits to Shetland for rounds of meetings there ably arranged by the sub-agent Basil Wishart.

The meetings in Orkney were nearly all well attended many full to capacity and sometimes as many as three in an evening. I marvelled at Jo's unflagging energy addressing meeting after meeting. He warned me that I would have to listen to much the same speech over and over again, but each time he began at a different point and came round full circle, all "off the cuff" without a note. His speeches were made without criticising or debunking his opposing candidates but keeping to his own policies all with good humour and occasionally brushing aside his wayward forelock. Though most of the meetings were well attended I remember our meeting in North Hoy School - a sparsely populated area. We failed to arrange a chairman beforehand but the local laird, Mr. Malcolm Stewart who came along agreed to officiate. Alas on taking the chair he announced that he was a Tory supporter. That notwithstanding, Jo proceeded to give a full address to an audience consisting of the chairman, the school caretaker, the boatman, my brother-in-law on holiday from Edinburgh and myself. Never was so much delivered by one to so few. A meeting in St Margaret's Hope ended late and we set off for home around midnight to cross the Churchill Barriers in a howling gale sending heavy spray across the roadway and enveloping the car. Jo thought that was great fun but I was fearful that the car engine might be flooded and stop and we would be swept over and into the sea. I kept the engine running fast in low gear and got across.

We arrived at the cottage in Harray where Jo was staying at that time and I watched him staggering into the gale and pulling his way along the wall to reach the door. But wind and weather did not deter Jo and next day he was back on the rounds, fresh as a daisy.

Other incidents and anecdotes are too numerous to relate in my short account but are to me unforgettable. The campaign continued but Jo never presumed the success that followed. Jo promised that if he were elected he would reside in Orkney. When he was elected he duly purchased the Manse in Firth where he and Laura made their home and brought up their children.

In addition to family and other commitments Laura was elected as a member of Orkney Islands Council in which she was an able and popular councillor:

Jo's parliamentary career is history. When he became our M.P. it never ceased to amaze me that he, a comparative stranger to these islands, so quickly understood and attended to his constituents' problems and dealt with them effectively.

Though honours and elevation to the House of Lords deservedly followed they did not alter Jo. Rank did not affect him in any way; he wore it modestly: He could walk with Kings but still remained Jo to all who knew him and so he will remain to us.

For my own part I was proud and privileged to have known Jo, a gentleman in the truest sense, and to have played a small part in his elections.

We shall miss him greatly.

We may not see his like again.

John M Robertson, Stromness.

Tribute to Laura at her Funeral
February 1994
by Howie Firth

Laura Grimond came from one of the most outstanding political families in the British Isles. Her grandfather was Herbert Henry Asquith, Prime Minister from 1908 to 1916 in a great reforming government whose benefits continue into the present day.

She grew up in a household which sparkled with ideas and intellect. Her father, Sir Maurice Bonham Carter, had been Asquith's private secretary; her mother, Lady Violet, was Asquith's daughter, and the young Bonham Carters were able to spend Christmases and other times of the year with their grandfather. He used to treat them as adults, and the discussions often included the common bond of a love of books.

The children's education was broad and varied, under the teaching of several governesses, which left additional time for more reading and subsequently travel. Laura spent time in Vienna and Paris before her coming-out season as a debutante.

She was very beautiful, and immensely full of life, and the photographs in the family album include one of her climbing a high tree, and another of her playing leapfrog and jumping high in the air over Mr. Asquith's second wife, Margot. It must have been quite clear that the man who was going to marry her would have to have a brilliance and a style of his own, and the young Jo Grimond had all of that. There was a slight pause while Lady Violet wondered whether Jo's prospects in the world should be carefully weighed up, and Sir Maurice was deputed to take him aside for a discussion on the subject. Fortunately, however Sir Maurice kept the conversation entirety to other matters, and Jo and Laura were married in 1938.

Jo Grimond found his whole family of in-laws fascinating for their sheer glorious vitality and style. They had, he observed, "a streak true Asquithian colour ' , with mental sinew, intellect and above all a tremendous characteristic of total loyalty, which became even stronger when the going got tough. Laura soon had to show her resourcefulness when the War took Jo away to the army and she had to leave London and live in various parts of the country. She was just out of her teens and between short visits together she had to cope with wartime conditions, look after members of their families, and then bring up their own children .

She was a natural writer, and her letters to Jo were full of detail and incident and above all vitality and humour. A wonderful humour that overarched everything else with a kind of dashing panache was a family characteristic. It was a part of a joy in life but also of a resilience that strengthened them in time of adversity. That resilience and humour was to be drawn on even further when Jo's future turned towards politics, and Orkney and Shetland in the 1945 election.

Jo did not expect to win, but Orkney and Shetland warmed to him to the extent that he was less than four hundred votes short of victory, and so the long haul then began to make sure of the 1950 election, which took him into Parliament. The work to cover the constituency, both in those election campaigns and throughout his subsequent career in Westminster, was immense and one of the keys to victory was the work carried out by Laura. She knew that success depended on detail, on planning election itineraries, on fundraising, on organisation and timing, and with the family characteristic of total loyalty and commitment, she put her energies into building from the base upwards, and whatever the task, she led by example.

In those election campaigns, each island had to be visited, by steamer or small boat, and there was a sense of adventure about a campaign which involved Foula and Fair Isle and Papa Stour. There were parts of the constituency where virtually the whole population would turn out to hear all the candidates, and there were other areas where only one person ever went along, to grill each candidate in detail and then faithfully report back the verdict to the rest of the Community. Everywhere had to be visited. Jo's rapid advance in national politics meant that Laura had increasingly to speak in her own right, and her clarity of thought and sheer lucidity of argument showed that she had inherited all the political flair of her family.

It was characteristic of her that what was memorable about it all to her was not the sheer amount of time and energy that she gave: instead she savoured the opportunity that she had to enjoy people and events. It was a time when elections in Orkney and Shetland were fought with great colour and style. There were supporters like the man in Finstown who was wont to divide the world into two categories, the Liberals who were "staunch", and the Tories, who were "rank". There were hecklers whose remarks became the stuff of legend, to be joyously retold to family and friends.

The delight in humour was part of the great bond that ran so deep between Laura and Orkney and Shetland. Her family traditions of brilliant wit found a kindred community where stories of characters and worthies were savoured and where even the greyest and wettest winter's day could be lit up by a gem of a remark. A gleam would come into her eye, and the start of a laugh, and you could suddenly see the enchantment that had been there all her life and which makes some people never seem to grow old.

She had a wonderfully elegant way of summing things up, and putting them in perspective. "All piers," she told an appreciative audience on sea transport in Kirkwall in March 1969, "come in three sorts. There are some that go too far into the sea, some that go too far out of the sea and some that never reach the sea at all." She prefaced the discussion by telling the audience that she approached the subject of piers with considerable hesitation, as in her experience they were places where angels feared to tread. At the beginning, no one could be brought to agree on where they should be sited. And once they had begun nobody could predict or knew where they were going to end.

She had a very deep feeling for landscape and buildings, which never left her. It combined the eye of the artist with the belief that people deserved to live in pleasant surroundings. Leading again by example she put immense energy and effort into a series of successful conservation projects. There was the establishment of the Hoy Trust and the purchase and restoration of the Strynd houses. Without her

Papdale House would have become bottoming for the modern school hostel and the now highly useful old Stromness Academy building would be no more.

Laura's campaigns were always fought with tenacity and flair, as a General would hold the line and skillfully deploy his troops. The fight to save Papdale House looked about as uphill a struggle as you could get, but she brought in Magnus Magnusson and Maurice Lindsay and the poet Sir John Betjeman, whose feelings for the beauty of old architecture and the barbarities of the new equalled her own. He arrived in Orkney on a day described by Jo as "one of those dreich days when the sky seems to be on the roof and every bush is shrivelled with wind, salt and rain – days known in Orkney as coorse". Sir John was, however, utterly undaunted by the weather and utterly entranced by the view, and his readings of his own poetry at the Concert in aid of the newly formed Orkney Heritage Society were spell-binding.

In all this work, Laura was looking not just at the past for its own sake but at enabling a future generation to enjoy it. The Hoy Trust, she emphasised was there to preserve the magnificent scenery of the area, certainly, but it was first and foremost for the people who lived there. And the greatest cause of all was simply other people, taking up the case of those with problems, visiting those who were ill or handicapped or with someone to look after, finding time to introduce someone to others of kindred interest, writing to encourage someone through time of difficulty, putting in a word for someone who needed help. She helped as an individual, and she helped as an MP's wife, and she helped through serving as an office-bearer for numerous organisations like the Guides and Women's Guild and many many more. She served with distinction for six years as Orkney Islands Councillor for Firth and Harray during which time she chaired the Social Work and Housing Committee with ability and compassion.

In her determination to help others through the world and put their welfare above her own, she was rather like one of the noblest and finest characters in Scottish literature, the schoolmaster in James Bridie's play "Mr Gillie": what happened to one's self was utterly unimportant - the real satisfaction in life was helping others to bring out the best in themselves.

Latterly her illness limited her efforts towards the various causes she had worked so hard for. She heard the good news of progress on St Boniface Church In Papay but knew that there were more buildings to be saved; she saw the Orkney Mental Health Association building up from the solid foundation she had put so much work into laying, but knew how much needed to be done to help so many carers;

and having so often run a stall for the "Save the Children" Fund at the St Magnus Fair and the County Show, she shared the deep anguish of many people at the suffering of the people of Bosnia and the all too limited assistance from the western world so far. She would, I am sure, be quite embarrassed that people were gathered together here to listen to an account of her own life and much rather want everyone to think instead about the work of these various organisations for whom today's collection will be given.

She died on February 15th, exactly 66 years after her grandfather. The Earl of Oxford and Asquith, and the epitaph written for him by a newspaper editor of the day would apply to her just as, accurately. "No man who ever played a great part in affairs was more conspicuously free from the common vices of public life.... His loyalty to his colleagues was one of his most striking attributes.... He will live in history as a type of all that is best in the English character." To which we would add - and the Orcadian character as well. She will be missed very much, but she leaves behind an enormous amount of good that many, many others will benefit from for a very very long time.

Tribute to Laura at the Memorial Service
St. James's, Piccadilly. 10.5.94
By Roy Jenkins

There are many here today whose memories of Laura go back further than mine. I did not know her as a child in the twenties when she and the other Asquith grandchildren were relegated on holidays to the dormitory of the elegant Mill House, while Margot and HHA mysteriously preferred the much less architecturally distinguished Wharf. Nor did I know her as a Liberal "girl" in the 30s an early product of that remarkable governess, Cuffy Hubler who managed to combine the running of the most respectable of seminaries for young ladies with living, on the premises, in sin with Foxy Falk, whose name pinpointed a personality which bore distinct traces of both Maynard Keynes and Thomas Balogh.

Yet I feel I can recapture something of the Laura of those days from the vivid and beautiful pictures of her at that time. There can hardly have been a girl who produced more unforgettable photographs. Several of them were reproduced with her obituaries. There was the extraordinarily vitality of her jumping over Margot Oxford, never an easy feat to perform. There was the 1938 marriage photograph, with Jo looking uncharacteristically glossy, but the result being one of the most evocative wedding pictures I have ever seen. There was a much later one in a boat in Orkney, and there was one of Jo, also rather uncharacteristically I would have thought, doing up the hooks on Laura's dress, no doubt at some Liberal Assembly conference hotel.

By the time I had come to know Laura (and Jo) quite well and greatly to value her approbation for something I had said or done or written. Although it was decades before the Alliance, the political gulf between us was never wide, and I very much liked her approval. She liked serious, taut, sharp, political conversation, in the appetite for which I, like her grandfather, have sometimes been regarded as deficient. Yet I always wanted to talk to her. I recall from a much later period of summer parties on a Thames-side lawn with several hundred people present. Never one went by, if Laura was there, as she mostly was unless Orkney called too insistently, without my moving at some stage, like a fish in its pre-ordained river course to Laura and not leaving her until I had been refreshed, amused and had my opinions on the main issues of the day burnished and reinforced.

Laura was married for 55 years to Jo, a politician of unique charm and self-deprecating wit. He was a dazzling companion and exciting leader. He never had power yet he never substituted bombast. He could at once slightly mock and inspire an audience. I shall never forget his speech at the fringe meeting of 2000 – some fringe- at Llandudno in 1981 when he both did these two things and gave his blessing to the Alliance.

But in the shade of such a tree, it cannot have been altogether easy for Laura to strike the right balance between spousely support and the maintenance of a distinct, discriminating and independent personality. Yet that she undoubtedly achieved. She managed to combine an undimmed commitment to her chosen causes with an unusual ability to prick any bloated bladders of nonsense.

As I began with Laura in her fashionable youth, so I end with a memory of her distributing polling day leaflets from 5.00am onwards on a wet morning at Warrington and eight months later on a cold morning in Hillhead. She did not do things by halves.

Her debilitating stroke at the end of 1992 was to me as surprising as it was tragic. With her spare and active body and vigorous mind she looked to my inexpert eye to be set for decades. No doubt it was better when the deep twilight set in, that it was not too prolonged. But the loss of both the Grimonds within a season leaves an immense gap to which their respective contributions were both equal and separate.

Tribute to Jo at the Memorial Service
St. James's, Piccadilly. 10.5.94
by Mark Bonham-Carter

First may I insert a postscript to Roy Jenkins's eloquent and vivid tribute to my sister Laura. The Laura I will remember, the Laura I will miss is the Laura of my childhood Laura my heroine - the skinny, mischievous, physically reckless, talented child who climbed trees and loved drawing, who played cricket and ran. And she ran very fast. She won the sisters' race at my private school three times in a row, prompting the headmaster, W. B . Harris, to write to my mother in his inimitable style:
"Golly that girl can shift! She must be the fastest sister we've had since Bunny Raven's." (Bunny Raven, who subsequently became Dean of King's College, Cambridge, had three sisters and I don't know which was Laura's rival).

And shift she did from then on - from clever athletic child to admired (but never dazzled) debutante, to marry (transitive verb) Jo Grimond, to become the mother of four, and then campaigner, candidate, election agent and councillor .

It was through her that I met Jo - husband and father: Member of Parliament: Liberal: collector of pictures: Rector of the Universities of Aberdeen and Edinburgh: Chancellor of the University of Kent: gardener: journalist: Scottish patriot and Orcadian: born St. Andrews July 29th 1913, died Orkney October 24th 1993.

I have been asked to say a few words about Jo. "Never", he used to say, "ask me to say 'just a few words' I give you a speech, a lecture, write an article at the drop of a hat, but 'just a few words' is much too difficult. " And how in "just a few words" can I evoke this man who represents so much we yearn for? So much we have lost? So much we need? On the one hand style, humour , self-deprecation; irreverence, on the other a sense of direction, values, liberalism, courage and flair.

He considered his career a failure. He was not quite the happy warrior he appeared. Politics for him was not simply an agreeable occupation for an amateur. On the contrary , despite his well-known aphorism that "it is preferable to be governed by Lord Melbourne than by Lenin" , he saw politics as a road to power and power to carry out policies he believed in. If some people underestimated his will to power, they were wrong. It is difficult to measure in an era when this country has not been overwhelmed with political talent, how much we have lost because Jo Grimond never had the opportunity to hold office and how much he lost by the same deprivation.

He found the Liberal Party dead on its feet and he breathed new life into it. In 1955, one year before he became Leader, there were six Liberal MPs with 2.5% of the vote. The picture is rather different today, and for that he is largely responsible. Without him the Liberal Parliamentary Party would have died. He knew that small parties cannot make opportunities but they can, given skill and courage and flair, take them. And Jo had skill and courage and flair. They can talk about the issues the big parties find too hot to handle and that was what he did, to take three examples, in the case of Europe, Scottish home rule and the realignment of the Left, twenty-five years before the Gang of Four and the Alliance of which he said, so characteristically, on TV , "The thing's bound to be a great success because Jenkins is such a good Liberal and Steel such a good Social Democrat."
He blazed trails that others have followed and he did all this with no staff, no speech writers, no research assistants, no-one beyond his minder and secretary , the essential Catherine Fisher .

There have been few post-war politicians who could rival his capacity to inspire and dominate a large public meeting. He had, to use an over-used word, charisma. As David Steel has written: "Jo inspired a whole generation of people to come into politics." He was recognised in the streets throughout the land. He drew crowds about him.

He was a Pied Piper in more ways than one and not least in Orkney and Shetland, the islands to which he was so deeply devoted. Howie Firth, who at one time directed Radio Orkney and who in one election was Jo's SNP opponent, said on Jo's death. "To a whole generation of us, Jo Grimond was as integral a part of Orkney as Skara Brae or St. Magnus Cathedral." He went on "It is really this evening as if a light has gone out in the north."

What Howie Firth said was confirmed by the crowds who attended his funeral in St. Magnus Cathedral in Kirkwall on that sunny October day last year and heard the tribute paid by Jackie Robertson, his agent in Orkney, and Margaret Crossan's poem from Shetland. He loved his constituents and his constituency. He loved his house, the Old Manse of Firth, the pictures by Scottish painters that decorated its walls, the garden, the expeditions to Skara Brae, Scapa, Hoy and St. Magnus Cathedral.

The fact is that Jo's public and his private faces almost wholly coincided and that those of us who knew him before he became a public figure saw in the public figure the private person we knew. What was rare, and indeed pleasing, was that what attracted us to the private person attracted the public at large.

This was at the heart of his well-known charm. He was not a construct put together by some public relations firm. He was himself: intelligent, irreverent, brave, eloquent, speaking for all of us far better than we could speak for ourselves.

Though I cannot speak the accent, I quote from Margaret Crossan's tribute from Shetland:

> *We hae to tank him fir mony things*
> *Dat he has dune fir wis*
> *Bit maest o aa whit we laek best*
> *Is his happy weel kent face*
> *Lord Grimond o Firth dey caa him*
> *Wir pleased hit sood be so*
> *Bit here in da isles whaar we luv him*
> *He'll aye, be kent as Jo.*

Contributors: